The number of elderly people in our society is increasing, and is likely to continue to do so in the future.
C. Paul Brearley, an experienced social worker, firmly believes that social work with the elderly can be both interesting and worthwhile, and sets out possibilities for change in the whole area of provisions for the elderly.

Designed for the social work student and for members of other caring professions, this book provides a basic understanding of the needs of older people in society. It deals with the role of the old person in society and attitudes to old age, as well as the physical, emotional and social needs of the ageing individual. It shows that material resources and social work skills can make a great deal of difference to the quality of life and health of elderly citizens, and is concerned therefore not only with the process of ageing but also with the validity of techniques of social intervention against a background of limited practical resources for the elderly.

The Author
C. Paul Brearley received his B.A. in Politics from the University of Leicester and subsequently took an Applied Social Studies course at the University of Sheffield. Before taking up his present position as Lecturer in Geriatric Social Work at the University of Southampton, he was a Principal Social Worker with the Nottinghamshire Social Services Department.

Social Work, Ageing and Society

LIBRARY OF SOCIAL WORK

GENERAL EDITOR: NOEL TIMMS

Professor of Applied Social Studies
University of Bradford

Social Work, Ageing and Society

C. Paul Brearley

Department of Sociology and Administration
University of Southampton

Routledge & Kegan Paul

London and Boston

First published in 1975
by Routledge & Kegan Paul Ltd
Broadway House, 68-74 Carter Lane,
London EC4V 5EL and
9 Park Street,
Boston, Mass. 02108, USA
Set in 10 on 11pt Pilgrim
and printed in Great Britain by
Northumberland Press Limited, Gateshead

ISBN 0 7100 8184 7 (c)
      0 7100 8185 5 (p)

Contents

Preface

Working with older people and the social deprivations which they often suffer can be an unhappy, depressing experience. Although this book looks at the many difficulties of bringing about change in the lives of the elderly through social work intervention it is chiefly a book about possibilities for change. Improvements can be made in their circumstances through an appropriate use of material resources and of social work skills.

Change, however, is usually only brought about after careful assessment and patient, hard work. It is not my intention to make the work look easy but to suggest that involvement with elderly clients can be interesting and worthwhile, and that change is at the very least a possibility.

My thanks are due to all those colleagues who have provided support and ideas, and also to the secretarial staff of the Sociology Department at Southampton University for their help with typing. I wish particularly to thank Miss C. M. Forsyth for helping me to begin thinking about the needs of older people, Mr E. G. Culham for allowing me to try out my ideas, Professor M. R. P. Hall for encouraging me to continue thinking, and my wife for putting up with this book for so long.

I

Introduction

With the drawing together of local authority social services in 1971 it might have been hoped that older people would receive an enthusiastic and understanding service. The range of knowledge of family situations, of admission to care, and of the whole span of human development held in a family-orientated department should have been much wider than in the previous narrowly defined specialities.

Some evidence suggests that this has not been so and that young, newly trained social workers feel less enthusiasm for working with the elderly, or chronically handicapped client than with children, or with relationship difficulties (Neill, 1973). This reflects a general attitude to work with the elderly which exists not just in the social work profession but also among other professionals concerned with caring for people. The stereotyped view of older people is that they only need adjustment to their environmental situation in order to remain happy—or at least in order to stay out of the way of the rest of the world. The social work assumption has often been that growth is an inappropriate concept in relation to old age. The inevitable follow-on to this assumption is a presentation of help based on a static concept of old age, taking no account of the continuous nature of the ageing process.

Our society has no functional place for the old, and we have created few acceptable roles for the elderly. The resources that are made available to help them to cope with the end of their life are inadequate, and few ways are open for older people to make use of the experiences they have gathered in earlier life.

Many questions need to be examined: Does old age exist? What is the ageing process? What does social work aim to do for older people? What do ageing people need? How valid is the assumption that older people need only material aid? How much scope is there for helping older people to grow and change? The list is endless —perhaps some of the questions can be answered.

ATTITUDES AND THE ELDERLY

The problem of attitudes to the elderly is one that hinders many attempts to improve services for older people. Geriatric medicine has only recently been recognised as a branch of medical teaching that merits the establishment of specialist Chairs of Geriatric Medicine. The low status of medicine in the care of the elderly has also meant that nursing older people has been seen as less important, or requiring less skill than nursing younger patients. Social work has suffered from the same kind of problem.

Butler (1969) has described some of the problems that exist in America in relation to old age:

(i) A personal revulsion to, and distaste for, growing old. This is perhaps the most important reason for many of the difficulties of attitudes to ageing. The individual who is growing old represses his feelings about late life and by doing so gains a temporary sense of mental security (Rudd, 1967). As a result of this repression, the presentation of that which is feared, in an ageing person causes distress and rejection. This process of 'elder-rejection' underlies behaviour towards older people.

(ii) A fear of powerlessness, uselessness and death. The fear of physical change, of the deterioration that ageing is expected to bring, and of death, is another important factor in the attitudes of professional workers.

(iii) Mandatory retirement removes the elderly from the mainstream of life: the economic system usually demands the withdrawal of an individual's active participation, regardless of his competence.

(iv) Vulnerability to robbery.

(v) Old people are seen as undeserving if they have been improvident, even if they have had no opportunity to save. Another side of the coin, in this country, is that those who have saved are often expected to pay for any services they receive, whilst those who have no money are 'rewarded' with free help (or perhaps 'degraded' by free help?).

(vi) Rehoused elderly come from the 'slums' and 'these people won't be able to afford better housing'.

The climax of life is reached before retirement for most people and the time after this is seen by many as a time of decline. Fear of death, increased physical incapacity, vulnerability, poverty, are all part of the stereotyped expectation of old age. Words like 'undeserving', 'revulsion', 'rejection', 'powerlessness', are expressions of repressed fear of old age.

The first, and most important, problem of working with the elderly is therefore the need for a change in attitudes. 'Old people' may be a useful term for the statistician who needs to collect information about a group: in the sense that they have all lived for the same number of years people over 65, or over 75, have something in common. They will have other things in common: ageing brings 'normal' physical, intellectual, and emotional changes that are shared by most people who live long enough. However, each individual follows his own way of life within those general changes. In the individual sense there is no such thing as old age, but only individual people, each at a point in the ageing process. Each one has his own needs and wishes, and has the right to decide what he wants from his remaining life. For social workers to deal in stereotyped approaches is to deny individual old people this right.

CAUSES OF STRESS

A lack of respect for work with the elderly is not only a function of the workers' feelings about old age; there are many real and potential sources of stress. The demand for resources is great. Residential, hospital, and domiciliary resources for the elderly are under continual pressure and social workers are pushed into making surface assessments knowing that they can only make inadequate provision. Stress, and feelings of guilt at being unable to solve, or even dare to look for problems is almost unavoidable in this situation. At the same time families will often only demand help for their older relatives when they are absolutely at breaking point. At such a time of crisis bitterness, argument, and conflict are frequent and the worker who gets caught up in such a crisis will experience anxiety and conflict himself.

In forming relationships with the individual older person difficulties of communication—because of sensory loss, or linguistic, social, or cultural factors—may exist. Working with an isolated and withdrawn, or hostile, aggressive, or probably demented old person does present difficulties and patience is essential. Depressed older people may help to create unhappiness and distress in the social worker.

A further aspect is that elderly clients do die: it is not easy to see death as a success for social work treatment. Social workers may fear any more than a superficial relationship with an elderly client because of the grief and distress that may attend the eventual death of the client.

Tension and stress is inevitable in providing help for older people. Some difficulties are inherent in the nature of the work, others are caused by inadequate resources, as well as the inappropriate use of resources. Learning to accept these difficulties is the first step to understanding the total needs of the older client and the impact that the ageing process makes on him.

SOCIAL WORK OBJECTIVES

Before looking at the specific objectives of social work with ageing clients it is necessary to review the current social work position. Social work theory and practice is developing rapidly over a range of skills and services. The traditional practice of casework has been challenged and criticised by those who advocate the use of group work skills, action for community change and development, etc.

One view of casework (Baker, 1972) suggests that there is a clear distinction between the use of the term casework in a loose sense and its more precise meaning. Social welfare work will involve the provision of material resources in a concerned way to improve the quality of life of individuals, and the haphazard use of personal contact between the social worker and the client in a spasmodic and relatively unplanned way. More precisely, casework can be defined as an ongoing relationship between worker and client that is used consciously and deliberately to help the individual in his environment. This help may include the provision of practical resources to assist with the problems that are important to the client. Even more narrowly, casework has been defined as consisting essentially of giving the client a very specific kind of interpersonal experience—activity directed to helping clients overcome problems involving difficulties in relating to people (Woodmansey, 1972).

For a long time caseworkers have claimed to have solutions for many forms of social problems but a lack af clarity about aims and objectives as well as inadequacy of information about effectiveness has led to a need to re-examine the nature of casework. The sensitive development, use and perception of a relationship that will help the whole individual towards autonomy in integrating his own needs with his external situation is one social work approach. It is currently an approach that is under highly critical review and reappraisal. In addition to the use of the dyadic casework relationship there has been an increase of interest in group work techniques. Social workers are using group relationships and group processes in order to bring about change. Beyond this social workers are also active in wider community contexts.

4

Community work is a function which is exercised by many different people as part of their professional task. It is essentially concerned with affecting the course of social change through the analysis of social situations and the formation of relationships with different groups (Gulbenkian Report, 1968). The Gulbenkian Report goes on to suggest that community work has three main aims: the democratic involvement of people in playing an active part in the running of their daily lives; the value of personal fulfilment in belonging to community; and the need to focus on the relationships of people's needs and problems rather than examining a series of problems in isolation from each other.

Here, then, are some of the trends of social work thinking. On the one hand casework techniques aim at the individual in his situation. On the other hand the community worker aims to affect the wider social background which takes account of the inter-relationships of individual problems but makes the individual himself a more shadowy participant.

However, to describe social work in this way is to present a flat picture with an unreal perspective. In the real-life social work situation the social worker is using a variety of skills and methods of intervention to meet the variety of human needs. The intervention may take many forms, from the provision of meals-on-wheels, to the use of a casework relationship, and the stimulation of radical social action.

At a time of such rapid change, when social work can mean so many things, it is hardly surprising that colleagues in other caring professions, as well as clients, find it hard to understand the basic tasks and objectives of social work. Younghusband (1973) has suggested that 'social work seems to me to have a threefold aim in relation to social ills which are remediable if we had the will to act. The first is to give help in terms of tomorrow morning to individuals and families who are suffering from such ills; the second is to press for better provision for them; and the third is to study causes and make the case for large-scale action.'

The social worker is concerned with facilitating social change on a number of levels. Fundamentally, therefore, he will need information and knowledge about behaviour in social situations: this knowledge will come from the social and behavioural sciences. This is obviously not a suggestion that social workers should try to know everything about behaviour; nor is it, necessarily, advocating generic work. It does seem, however, that social work training should introduce the social worker to the meaning of human behaviour and social interaction, and to the implications of intervention both in individual and in large-scale social situations.

5

In considering the objectives and tasks of the social worker concerned with an ageing client two basic assumptions will be made:

(i) social workers are concerned with the alleviation of stress through intervention in situations of social dysfunction;

(ii) social workers must be flexible in the presentation of resources during that intervention.

The amount of flexibility will be partly dependent on the nature of the problem, partly on the availability of resources, and partly a reflection of the background and temperament of the worker himself. Each social worker will ultimately tend to use the particular body of knowledge with which he is most familiar, and, within that, the knowledge that makes most sense to him as an individual.

SOCIAL WORK AND AGEING

In working with ageing clients, the social worker can draw on a wide range of skills to meet the needs that are presented. Some needs are more commonly presented by older clients and these are primarily concerned with situations of loss and subsequent adjustment. Each individual client will present his own unique needs in a unique environment and will consequently require an individual solution. A number of general aspects have been frequently raised in the allocation of services to older people.

The current approach to providing care for the elderly is based on the assumption that all older people have a right to remain independent. It is not always plain what is meant by 'independence'. Often it seems to refer to the right of the individual to remain in his own home for as long as possible. It is hard, however, to describe as independent a housebound old lady who relies on a daughter to do her shopping, a neighbour to do her cooking, and a home help to do the cleaning. In this physical sense of independence it is likely that an old lady in an Old People's Home who has her own room, can walk to the dining room, dress herself, and get out to church each week, will feel that she enjoys more independence.

In another sense, to remain in her own home may give the old lady a greater feeling of self-direction and control over her total life activities. She may have to rely on someone to empty the commode for her but at least she can pay her own milk bill and her own rent man. A more suitable word than independence might be individuality. To maintain individuality the elderly client has a right to a degree of self-determination, in so far as his wishes and needs are compatible with those of others around him, and a right to dignity and respect. This will include physical independence but for many of the elderly clients who come to the notice of social workers this cannot realistically be achieved because of physical or mental deterioration.

A further objective of social work with ageing clients should be the recognition of the right to continue growing and changing. There are problems about over-emphasising the growth content of the ageing process which will be examined later but it is extremely important that the elderly client should be allowed the opportunity to change. A person who is seventy years old may have another fifteen or twenty years of life, or perhaps more. Considerable change may occur in that time, and facilitating the process of ageing will involve an acceptance of continuing change.

The achievement of satisfaction in old age is linked to this acceptance. Ageing is a process in which we are all involved and satisfaction implies the continuance of the process. Social workers concerned with the problems of ageing should aim to overcome the obstacles to change and progress, and success implies the restoration of process.

Satisfaction in old age is also linked to an acceptance of the life that has gone before. Social work is aimed at the achievement of an integration of the past, present and future of the individual. Seeing a pattern in the past helps to identify the inevitability and accept-ability of the present, and ultimately the acceptance of death. Social work with ageing clients is therefore concerned with the main-tenance of a process of ageing that recognises the needs of each individual to progress, at whatever age they may be. The right to individuality, respect and dignity are a fundamental part of the achievement of satisfaction in old age.

One other important aspect is that of family involvement. Two of the commonest assumptions are that families have a duty to care for their elderly relatives, and that most families reject this duty. The reality is that most families accept that they have a duty to care, and will often continue to do so beyond the point of reason. As far as possible social workers should involve the family and the community in help for the elderly client, not because of a real or imagined moral or statutory duty, but because the problems of the individual old person are inextricably linked to those of the people around him. Ignoring the family may cause greater problems in the long run, especially in terms of the guilt that is aroused if children cannot care for ageing parents.

In achieving these objectives several fundamental tasks can be identified.

(i) Assessment of the total needs of the client is of paramount importance. Stereotyped attitudes, stress, and other factors that will also be discussed have too often led to a hurried look at the surface needs of older people. The first contact between the social worker and his elderly client contains elements of both the collection of information on which to base treatment and of treatment itself. If that first contact fails to offer understanding of the client's needs then information that is given will be inadequate. The whole programme of social work intervention with the older client rests on an understanding of normal ageing processes and of the problems and difficulties that are likely to arise for the ageing individual.

(ii) Communication will also be a fundamental task if assessment and treatment are to begin. Many problems exist in establishing effective channels of communication with older people. Failing eyesight and hearing make simple conversation more difficult. Sometimes the loss of speech or the loss of ability to understand the speech of others are the result of a stroke or illness, and patience is essential to overcome these problems. Social workers may need to use a wider range of techniques of communication with older clients if relationships are to be established.

(iii) Relationships are the main basis of all social work treatment. The establishment of mutual trust and understanding in order to help individuals and groups to a situation of greater self-direction and personal integration is essential. Work with ageing clients, again, has particular aspects. Loss, dependence, family relationships, environmental deprivations, etc., all take on particular importance in some aspects as people grow old.

(iv) Providing practical aid has usually been the first resort of social workers in helping the elderly. This is certainly very important—old people as a group are deprived of money, housing, social support, etc.—but giving material aid should be carefully considered. It will only be relevant as part of a wider treatment plan for the ageing individual; it is not an end in itself.

These four tasks—assessment, communication, forming relationships, and providing practical help—will be used as the basis of an examination of the needs and services for the elderly. It is important to remember in considering them that one of the paradoxes of social work in ageing is that social work is primarily problem-orientated and work with ageing must be primarily process-orientated. This book is about the reconciliation of problem-solving techniques with the need of most older clients for the restoration of a normal process of ageing.

POPULATION—THE REASONS FOR CONCERN

The reasons for increasing demand for services of all kinds from older people are well known but some misperceptions can be clarified and explained.

The principal problem is that there are more older people around. At the beginning of the twentieth century 6·2 per cent of the total population was over retirement age. In other words there were less than two and a half million people over retirement age in a population of over thirty-eight million. Since then the proportion over retirement age has risen to 16 per cent and is expected to continue to rise to 16·8 per cent by 1981 (Central Statistical Office, 1972). After the 1980s this trend begins to fall off, and by the year 2011 projections suggest that the proportion of older people will be down to 15·2 per cent. This is mainly due to an increase in the younger working ages.

The implication of these figures is that in the past the relative impact of older people on the total social situation was much less than it is now. Old people were around but could be absorbed by the larger number of younger people who were able to care for them.

The current picture is more complex. An increase in the proportion of older people has obviously been accompanied by a decrease in the proportion of younger people. A small but important decrease in the proportion of people between the ages of 15 and 64 (59 for women) means that there are relatively fewer people around to care for the dependent age groups. This picture will improve by the end of the century but the immediate situation is that there are not enough people working to provide care for those very young and very old people who need it.

This does not mean that people are living to be older; it does mean that more people are living into old age. The average expectation of life has increased remarkably from perhaps twenty years in Graeco-Roman times, and perhaps no more than thirty or thirty-two years in Norman, or Elizabethan England (Agate, 1970), to forty-eight years in 1901. In 1969 it had reached over sixty-eight years for the new-born child, and even a person of seventy can expect at least another nine years of life.

Not only does this imply a higher proportion of old people in present-day society but it also implies a higher proportion of very old people. There are more people over seventy-five and eighty and these are the people who are tending to put most strain on social services. Up to that age the majority of people are able to cope with the stresses and strains of life alone. After that age they begin to become more frail and therefore to be more dependent on others.

Another aspect of population change that has an important effect on the elderly is the fact that there are now fewer single women:

women are more likely to get married now than in the past. It was often the single daughter who stayed at home and looked after her parents in their old age and the change in marriage opportunities has had an important effect on this.

Similarly, there are now more job opportunities for women, so that daughters, married or unmarried, are often faced with a choice between greater income and the satisfaction of a job, and staying at home to care for elderly parents. A greater degree of mobility of labour has also contributed to the geographical division of some families and the scattering of support systems.

The total population picture, then, is that there are now more old people than there used to be in terms of the number of people available to care for their needs. In this sense there is 'a problem of old age'.

2

The normality of ageing

Although social workers tend to be concerned with minority problems (and therefore in a statistical sense, with abnormality), in terms of their objectives they are concerned very much with normality. Assessment and subsequent actions can only make sense if they are linked to aims. Although any discussion of normality raises issues of subjectivity as well as political and cultural aspects (which will be discussed later) it seems important to try to establish a picture of what ageing means for most people in our particular society.

SOCIAL AND PSYCHOLOGICAL ASPECTS

Growing older is, of course, a process in which we are all involved, even before birth. There are various socially determined highlights throughout the process—starting school, examinations, coming of age, and retirement are obvious examples. Less tangible but often of equal emotional significance are the vague colloquialisms—'life begins at forty', 'as old as you feel', or 'as young as you look'. Old age is rigidly and artificially socially defined by retirement—often a division between usefulness and rejection.

Roles and ageing

Bearing in mind that old age is an unreal concept and varies from individual to individual it is possible to see two trends in role allocation and the elderly.

(a) *The stereotypes*   The stereotype picture of the old person usually centres around a few specific traits—hypochondria, rigidity, a turning to the past, self-assertiveness, feelings of inadequacy and rejection, apathy, negativism, social withdrawal. The more charitable side of the coin sees the old person as determined to maintain high standards, often strict but dependable in times of trouble, loyal, and proud.

(b) *Active roles* As a group the elderly are poor, less likely than younger people to be working, and they are less likely to be physically active. Obviously in individual situations they are likely to be participating in a wide variety of social situations but will tend to be restricted by these three major considerations: economic, occupational and physiological. Other factors like social class level, degree of family integration, and availability of community links will also play a major part in how far the older person is able to maintain continuity of active roles.

There are limited opportunities for the ageing individual to learn how to behave as an old person. A child has many opportunities to experience behavioural expectations in social situations through interaction with family and friends, and at school. The individual who is growing older meets a decreasing number of situations in which he can interact with contemporaries. Sometimes, through ageing with a marriage partner, friend or sibling, some learning about the ageing process can take place and sometimes this can happen through social clubs for the elderly. Unfortunately, only a minority of old people are members of clubs, and reducing physical capacity and an increasing death rate among friends result in fewer and fewer chances for learning about other old people.

It is interesting that in our industrialised society we tend to value the experience of age only in a few occupations. The older politician who presents a role-model based on building up years of wisdom and experience has little in common with the alienated worker whose production-line skills are obsolete and devalued. It is hardly surprising, then, that the view of the ways in which old people can behave has to fall back on stereotype. We have none of the clarity of the primitive society in which the older craftsman passed on his craft and enjoyed power in consequence—or alternatively the uncomplicated disposal of feeble old men and women by migratory tribes. Our society provides a multiplicity of ways of ageing with few clear patterns.

Disengagement and involvement

Cumming and Henry (1961) have put forward a theory of disengagement in which they propose very firmly that ageing is essentially a process and that old age does not have a sharp cut-off point at retirement. They suggest that this process represents a two-sided interaction by which society as a whole makes increasingly fewer demands on each individual as he grows older and on the other hand the individual enjoys and encourages this withdrawal from involvement.

In a study in Kansas City they identified changes at a number of levels of interaction. They suggest first of all that there is a reduction in the variety of active roles of the ageing individual; that he will reduce the number of his interactions with others and also the variety of others with whom his interactions take place. Second, they identify a change in the density of interaction—a lowering of the amount of interaction with others of the type which will affect behaviour. Finally, in addition to a reduction in social life space (the actual total number of contacts with others) Cumming and Henry suggest that there is, with increased age, less ego-energy available for responding to the environment. In terms of disengagement theory, major life changes (widowhood, retirement, etc.) are seen as being coped with within a gradual process of adjustment; later life is a slow and satisfying withdrawal from the world, preparing the individual for death.

Debate on this theory has taken two other forms. Lowenthal and Boler (1965) have agreed that there is a reduction of social involvement but have queried how far this was voluntary on the part of the ageing person. Going further than this Havinghurst (1968) has agreed that for most people the process is not a two-sided, naturally accepted one but is in fact a one-sided imposition of a disengagement pattern on individuals. For some this may become a habitual way of life but for most, according to Havinghurst, it is not a self-chosen pattern.

There can be no doubt that ageing means that most people are involved in a loss of active roles. They stop being users of public transport, or people who have workmates, or colleagues; they usually lose many of the roles that attach to being in employment. It is perhaps easiest to believe that each individual adapts to life-changes in his own individual way, according to his own particular circumstances and in terms of his earlier-life adaptive patterns.

Personality adaptation

One interesting study of personality adaptation in later life was conducted in California by Suzanne Reichard and others (1962). This study was of a sample of men between the ages of 55 and 84; half were retired, half were still in full-time employment. Five main patterns of adjustment were identified, three described as 'successful', two as 'unsuccessful', and only a minority being placed in the three successful groups.

Mature or constructive men are involved in warm personal relationships and welcome retirement as an opportunity for more interaction. They have a sense of humour, are relaxed and enjoy hobbies. They are independent, but not rigid and are flexible and realistic in examining themselves. They look back on life with few regrets and forward with anticipation, with a calm acceptance of death. 'Rocking-Chair' or dependent men tend to be passive rather than active. They prefer to stay at home and are relatively un-ambitious. Retirement is welcomed as freedom from work. Usually they have dominant wives and although generally satisfied with the world, show tendencies towards unrealism, and over-optimism. The third group of 'successfully' adjusted men were the defensive or 'armored'. These men are rigid; over-controlled and bound by habit and convention. They tend to see few satisfactions in old age and look forward to it with some doubts. By remaining constantly active they avoid thinking about death.

In addition to these three groups Reichard's study points to two further, less acceptable patterns of adjustment. Angry men tend to blame their environment and are consequently hostile, suspicious, and aggressive in their behaviour towards others. Patterns of incon-sistency in their working background are common, as well as neurotic behaviour. Old age and death present an external threat and their reaction is resentment. The final group were the self-hating men who react by blaming not the outside world but them-selves. Depressive and poorly adjusted at work they reject their wives and despise themselves. They look forward to death as a welcome release from an unworthy existence.

Although dealing with a small sample, which included no women, this study does at least begin to demonstrate the obvious—that each person ages in his own individual way. Neugarten (1963) and others have emphasised this fact, that older people continue to be the kind of people they have been in earlier life. It is far too simplistic to suggest that there is one process of ageing: there are as many processes of ageing as there are ageing people.

Intellect and performance

In measuring changes in intellectual performance on an individual level it is impossible to draw any conclusion other than that there are immense variations. There are many who have been very capable and productive into their eighth and ninth decades while others have been 'worn out' at much younger ages. However, if groups of men and women are measured generalised trends can be noted.

Older people are more cautious and are less willing to advise a risky course of action than younger ones (Botwinick, 1966) and they see the world in less 'loving' terms than the young (Neugarten, 1963). It is also suggested that older people are more rigid in their thought (Chown, 1972) but this must be related to age-changes in intelligence. Cultural, educational, and generational variations make comments on intelligence in relation to ageing complex (Chown, 1972). There seems to be a decline in problem-solving ability, which is compensated for by an increase in learned response. The longer a person has been around the less likely it is that he will have to face new situations. Therefore, although he may not be as capable as he previously was of solving a new problem, he is more likely to have acquired the necessary learned skill to cope with it. In this sense there may be a loss of adaptability or an increased rigidity.

Ageing brings a slowing down of performance at all levels and it is commonly suggested that this is linked to a lack of motivation. The evidence for this is sparse and it has been demonstrated that older and younger people spend proportionately similar amounts of time on actually solving easy or difficult problems (Chown, 1972). It may be, however, that older people are more likely to abandon their attempt to solve a problem because they are slower and less able to master difficulties and they are more likely to accept an approximate solution—but this is not necessarily due to lack of motivation (Bromley, 1966). Given the time and opportunity to learn many older people can do so (Chown, 1972). However, there is a good deal of evidence that short-term memory becomes increasingly less efficient with ageing and this may in turn affect the ability to retrieve and select facts from the long-term memory.

In summary, the older person tends to be slower, less adaptable, but with a store of experience and learning with which to compensate for his losses. His memory, especially for recent events, is less efficient but given time he is able to learn.

A DEVELOPMENTAL APPROACH

There is no doubt that there are many dangers in over-emphasising the growth aspect of growing old. To do so tends to deny the satisfactions that lie in relaxation and lessening abilities. Paradoxically the achievement of a satisfying and graceful old age involves the individual in learning to adapt and adjust to deteriorating abilities. Nevertheless it is important to recognise that growing old is one end of a continuum which begins at conception, and the links between childhood and later life must not be neglected. From one stand-point progress through life is growing up; from another standpoint it is growing old. The development of personality involves a con-tinuous process of interaction between the individual and his environment. Developmental direction begins with genetic in-heritance and with influences inside the womb, and each stage of development has to be negotiated in terms of previous stages. In this sense old age is a function of all that has gone before.

The fundamental patterns of emotional behaviour and attitudes are acquired in early childhood. Psychoanalytical theories suggest that the basic formation of ego, super-ego, and ego-ideal takes place during the first few years of life. This development takes place because of the child's dependence on, and interaction with, his parents. Goldfarb (1965) has suggested that the majority of people remain in a large part dependent: dependency needs established in childhood become the chief motivation of the adult. He proposes that the life goal of each person is the search for, and the holding on to, someone who can be designated 'the helpful one'.

Characteristically the dependent person undertakes activities because he expects to gain the support of a parent-figure through them. The non-dependent person, contrastingly, carries out activi-ties because he gains satisfaction from the activities for their own sake. Dependency is a powerful socialising force in so far as individuals will act in a socially acceptable way in order to gain the support of the significant other person. This does not necessarily involve the dependent person in adopting a subservient position; indeed the search for dependence may involve taking up a control-ling approach. Patterns of interaction both on the level of intimate and of wider social relationships are a function of depending needs, according to Goldfarb.

His argument progresses in suggesting that the parent-surrogate figure need not overtly have objectively parent-like characteristics, although this may often be the case. Dependency-needs continue into middle and later life and changes brought about by the ageing process may affect the ways in which each individual is able to meet or seek satisfaction for his dependency-needs. It is likely, for example, that a spouse who is cast in the role of parent-surrogate will die. Alternatively, a crisis illness, such as a stroke, may alter dependency-needs. In such circumstances dependency-needs may be met through casting the children in the role of parent. Constant appeals for help, perhaps manifesting themselves through illness, may be made to test out the reliability of the relationship.

In this way dependency-needs acquired in very early life are re-awakened and realigned in later-life situations. It is easy to see the behaviour of the adolescent who seeks independence from the family while needing the security of his parents to fall back on mirrored in the behaviour of old people in institutions who demonstrate an ambivalence in their dependent role. The conflict between the need to retain individuality and to remain dependent on a supporting other is one that pervades the whole of life but is brought to the fore by particular events or processes; the deterioration that accompanies ageing is one such process.

From the viewpoint of object relations theory, loss and consequent anxiety play a considerable part in personality development. Through his adjustment and adaptation to situations of loss the child learns about himself in relation to his environment. Loss creates anxiety and arouses feelings of guilt and the way the child is able to handle these feelings dictates the ways in which he can face future losses. Ageing brings many loss situations for the individual: in facing up to these the ageing person will behave according to the ways in which he learned to function in earlier life.

In these important aspects of dependency and loss there are strong and definite links between early-life development and later-life behaviour. It is also possible to identify some defence mechanisms that make their presence more obviously felt with ageing.

Physical change in old age leads to a changing view of self, and physical deterioration means a shrinking self-concept. For some old people this seems to mean a feeling of helplessness and smallness in the face of a large, overwhelming world. This feeling is demonstrated and emphasised by increasing fear of road traffic, confusion over decimal currency changes, or increasing prices. This reduction in ego-functioning tends to lead to the emergence of projective mechanisms. We all tend to project the unacknowledged aspects of ourselves on to others, or on to the environment. Chronic senile brain changes commonly lead to an increase in this tendency but it also seems that normal ageing brings a similar increase in paranoid, persecutory feelings. These may take the form of arguing with friends over previously accepted details or habits, or it may be the projection of inner feelings of chaos on to the environment, the political situation, etc.

Linked with the feeling of external threat is the tendency to slip into regressive behaviour patterns. In their extremes these may be incontinence and chronic physical dependence but may more commonly be petulant, demanding, dependent behaviour. To some extent, also, reminiscence and day-dreaming may represent a regressive fantasising but this will be considered fully later.

Growing old and its attendant role-loss involves the older person in a loss of status. In denying this loss he may become excessively authoritarian with those who are close to him. Perhaps the origin of conflict between grandparents and younger children lies in an exaggerated reaction to this denial.

The capacity to tolerate difficulties, failures, disappointments, and crises in old age is related on many levels to early life. Research into reactions to parental deprivation has shown strong links between deprivation and the capacity to give and receive affection later. It seems fundamental to providing a social work service to the elderly to remember that an old person reacts in terms of earlier learned behaviour but all behaviour is subject to continuing changes in relationships and environment. At whatever stage of the life continuum he may be, each person is susceptible to change, and social work assessment must recognise that old age is not a static condition.

PHYSICAL ASPECTS OF AGEING

In considering physical changes it is important to distinguish those changes which take place as a result of the process of ageing and those problems which result from a gradual accumulation of illness. The process of biological ageing involves two parallel processes: that of growth and that of involution. During the early years growth predominates but involution gradually takes over, although the rate of ageing varies widely. As in other areas of functioning it is virtually impossible to delineate normality. Since there is little accumulated information about the height and weight of groups of normal older people it is difficult to set outside limits on what is usual, but generalised trends can be suggested.

Ageing brings a shortening of the spinal column because of shrinking and calcification of the inter-vertebral discs. Certain bones show characteristic changes with age, and ageing is characterised by a shortening of the trunk and a tendency to comparatively long extremities. Muscular changes show a loss of elasticity and atrophy associated partly with disuse and partly with loss of bulk and irreversible shrinking. Neuromuscular co-ordination is impaired and consequently movements are slower and not so precise as in younger people, and voluntary movements are progressively more difficult. Weight shows a tendency to increase during later middle age, reaching a plateau at about the age of 65-74 years, and then a fall in the years after that. Lymphoid tissues tend to reduce and be replaced by fat and fibrous tissue: redistribution of fat, especially from the face and to the abdomen and hips, takes place. Typically, then, the old person is slightly stooped, with comparatively long arms, weight-loss and redistribution of tissue, and with a general slowing of muscular response.

In addition to these major changes, other involutional changes take place. Hair-loss is a gradual process as follicles become fewer: this is especially true of men but many women begin to show some recession of hair by middle age. This loss is not restricted to the hair of the head: there is also a loss of the pubic and body hairs in the reverse order to that in which they grew. Greying of the hair, while not inevitable, is common and may occur early according to hereditary factors.

The eye and the ear also change from the age of 40-5 years; in the eye presbyopia—a form of long-sightedness—develops, along with a gradual reduction of the visual fields and a higher threshold for light stimulation. Characteristically, older people develop a gradually increasing high-tone hearing-loss and old people have particular difficulty in disentangling non-specific conversation, or conversation between several people.

There is also a generalised decline in organ function but it is often difficult to distinguish the physiological from the pathological. It seems likely, too, that there is a slowing down in the general metabolism. Unfortunately there is still insufficient information about normal groups and so it is often difficult to identify abnormality at various chronological stages.

Physical activity

One other important aspect of physical change in ageing is that of activity and exercise. Work by Dr Irene Gore (1973) has highlighted the relevance of physical activity in maintaining health in old age. Those people who continue to exercise, it is suggested, are far less likely to experience degenerative change. Some work in Russia and Eastern Europe has proposed that man is born with an inborn desire to move which increases as the child grows, flattens off in middle age and declines as the body ages. This decline can be slowed or halted by continued activity: the more the body is exercised the easier it is to remain active (Gore, 1972). This approach must be very relevant to the integration-segregation, disengagement-activity debate. How far are those people who appear disengaged only behaving in that way because, as a result of habitual disuse, they lack the physical energy to break out of their way of life? The work of Woodruff and Birren (1972) is also of interest: they suggest that characteristic levels of activity in old people show chronic adaptation, perhaps resulting from sensory deprivation, in turn resulting from the lack of environmental stimulus commonly experienced by the elderly. The central nervous system has a reserve plasticity, according to this theory, and external stimulation may be as important to physical well-being as continuing exercise.

Sexual activity might also be mentioned here; there is no physical reason why sexual activity should not continue into later life. The main controlling factors in the continuation of sexual intercourse into old age seem to be habit and regularity, preferably within a single stable relationship.

OCCUPATION, RETIREMENT AND ECONOMICS

It is impossible to review normal ageing without some consideration of occupational and economic change, although these will be discussed in more detail later. Retirement is usual, even though some people continue in full- or part-time employment after 65 : in 1971 19·3 per cent of men aged 65 and over were working, as were 16·1 per cent of married women, and 7·8 per cent of single women. For the majority of older people this insistence on retirement will mean a sudden change in financial status. Age Concern, a national voluntary body concerned with problems of older people, has drawn attention through a number of studies to the financial circumstances of the retired. These studies have highlighted in particular the reliance of the elderly on supplementary benefits and the inability of many old people to pay for basic necessities—food, warmth and adequate housing. In summary, it is because our industrial society expects people to retire at a particular age and does not value them sufficiently to allow them enough money for their needs that retirement commonly (if not necessarily normally) means poverty. This poverty is fundamentally a result of inadequate private resources (largely because of the late development of occupational pensions) and the failure of State pensions to fill the remaining gap.

AGE AND SATISFACTION

Up to 5 per cent of elderly people are in a long-stay institutional environment of some kind and about 13 per cent or 14 per cent are housebound. Here at least are some situations in which one might objectively feel that dissatisfactions might be common. Overtly, the ageing process brings an ever-increasing number of losses which might be difficult to connect with a continuing satisfaction. There is no doubt, however, that life at all ages has compensations and, if this is so, where do the satisfactions lie?

Margery Fry in *Old Age Looks at Itself* (1954) puts both sides of the problem :

> I have spoken of the pleasures of old age, and it would be
> ungrateful to deny that there are many which some,
> if not all, old people enjoy. Those who have learnt to live
> (on however a humble scale) amongst the things of
> the mind can follow them more peacefully when instinct
> and ambition and competition are less disturbing and
> when leisure is compulsory. But [she said] time plays us a
> dirty trick. With our retarded metabolism the days
> and weeks seem to race by, and even the number of
> hours in the day which we have the energy to use profitably
> grow fewer.

Looking closely for the meaning of the word 'satisfaction' only leads to more confusion, with 'happiness', 'desire' and 'gratification' beginning to creep in. From a rather negative approach satisfaction could be the absence of dissatisfaction. If this were so the vast majority of old people would appear to be satisfied—as a group, old people are apparently non-complainers. On the whole, for example, older people tend not to complain of ill-health, and they tend not to take notable political action to alter their economic circumstances. As individuals on the other hand their views will be very varied and anxieties are common. Once again it seems most suitable to suggest that satisfaction and happiness are very individual emotions. Each person sees his own life as unique and his attitudes are a function of his genetic endowment and environmental and interpersonal experience. Satisfaction for each of us is therefore a highly personal experience.

Erikson (1950) has contributed to the understanding of the situation in his consideration of ego-development. In the development of ego-identity Erikson proposes eight stages of integration. The negotiation of each stage of conflict demonstrates that the ego is at that time strong enough to integrate the required timetable of the organism with the structure of social institutions around it. The final stage that must be resolved (following from those of Trust versus Mistrust; Autonomy versus Shame and Doubt; Initiative versus Guilt; Industry versus Inferiority; Identity versus Role Diffusion; Intimacy versus Isolation; Generativity versus Stagnation) is that of Ego-Integrity versus Despair : the final achievement of an integrated state of mind. In Erikson's terms this involves several constitutional elements but principally it means an acceptance of an order and meaning in the totality of the individual's life—past, present and future. 'It is', he says, 'the acceptance of one's one and

21

only life cycle as something that had to be and that, by necessity, permitted of no substitutions.' Despair, as the conflicting tendency, represents the feeling that life is too short to make up the deficits in past life: it involves, in other words, the fear of death.

This concept of the achievement of maturity through the ultimate development of ego-integrity suggests another view of satisfaction. The person who can look back on life and see a clear, logical pattern in which good or bad events each have their place in the final order is arguably a satisfied person. This does not just mean that the contentment of maturity is backward-looking but it also involves seeing the present against the relevance of the past and finding meaning in both. From this safe stand the future, and the inevitability of death, can be viewed with acceptance rather than resignation or despair.

To reach this stage of integrated behaviour several people have suggested that there are essential prerequisites. Alastair Heron (1963) puts forward the following preconditions required for retirement to be a period of fulfilment: good physical and emotional health; adequate income, substantially beyond subsistence level; suitable accommodation; congenial associates and neighbours; one or more absorbing interests; an adequate personal philosophy of life.

Adequate adjustment will certainly be encouraged if internal and external stresses are reduced and if support is available, and the following factors seem particularly important:

(i) An integration of the past and present and an acceptance of an overall order and pattern to life.

(ii) A realistic acknowledgment of the inevitably of death and a recognition of the 'rightness' of death.

(iii) Adequate provision of physical necessities—housing, food, warmth, money, etc.: the criteria of adequacy will, of course, vary from individual to individual, and from group to group.

(iv) A sufficient amount of support from relationships to be able to enjoy the contentment of an essentially narcissistic drawing in to inner satisfactions.

It is tempting to add good health to this list but there are many chronically sick or disabled older people who have been able to reach a stage of integration that has little to do with their physical condition.

(v) Most important of all is the opportunity for each individual to obtain the necessary external environment to satisfy his unique inner needs.

The great majority of old people seem to reach a rather more than less satisfying level of adjustment. Contentment lies perhaps in being able to live a slower life, aimed increasingly at maintaining personal functions—a time for relying and depending on others but a time also for placid benevolence, for giving from a lifetime of experience.

Death

Normal is not an appropriate word to use in relation to death. Death, as an abstract, as an ending to conscious existence, is inevitable rather than normal. To define death is an impossible and fruitless task: the only certainty about death is that it is there and that it is an inescapable fact. The actual events leading up to death may themselves be classified as normal or abnormal but death cannot be classified.

In some of his later work Freud (1920) considered the instinct that leads us towards death. In an analytical sense death has a 'rightness' about it; it is a logical conclusion to the process of growth, development, and ageing. In every other sense death is right: in theological terms death is a step towards another existence; in demographic terms death is a balancing factor in social groups; and in physiological terms it is a conclusion to a slow process of bodily shrinkage.

Death itself is, then, unavoidable but in our present society the fear of death plays an important role. The symbolism attendant on grieving in more primitive cultures is now reduced and outlets for grief are consequently fewer. Death is a subject that is rarely discussed and the dead and dying tend to be hidden away. Anxiety about death plays an extremely important part in behaviour and although these anxieties rarely come to the fore in young people they are reported as becoming increasingly common as people grow older. It is relatively easy for a younger person to hide his fear, or to see it in less personal terms by worrying about elderly relatives, and friends. For the older person this is not so easy: most people in later middle-age will admit to thinking about death in personal terms, at least occasionally. Usually, however, what they fear is not death itself, but the pain that they expect to attend the dying (Hinton, 1967). Older people, over the age of about 75 years, are less likely to dwell on anxieties about death; possibly this is because they accept death or possibly they deny its existence because of intolerable anxieties.

Death, and the fear of death, are major considerations in looking at the process of ageing. The fear of death becomes commonly less pressing as the ageing person reaches a total 'view' of life, and death looms not as a frightening blankness, but as a logical conclusion.

SUMMARY

This brief review of the process of normal ageing will, hopefully, have begun to reveal the complexities of reaching a definition of normality. In our current state of knowledge this definition has to be a collection of subjective impressions measured against a few facts and many theories—often unsubstantiated.

The normal old person seems to be someone who plays out his life within the limitations of the roles society ascribes to him, as he perceives them. As he grows older his body changes, he becomes weaker and slower, stooped, wrinkled, and often greying. He is less adaptable, and more cautious, he takes longer to learn new things, and his memory is beginning to be less efficient. What is certain is that he grows old as he has grown up—in his own unique, individual way. Some older people want fewer relationships, require a less active participation in the world; others want to remain active contributors but are unable to do so because of social pressures; others do continue to play an important part. The normal older person reacts in his own way to ageing for many reasons: early-life developmental factors, combined with later experiences of people and environment, as well as inherited factors, create his behaviour patterns. He reacts as he does because of all these factors and because of the society in which he lives.

Above all, ageing is a process: it is a process of change in which we are all involved. In beginning to think about social work with older people this is the first fundamental fact—that old age is just one end of the continuum that begins in childhood. The second factor is that old age—if it exists at all—is not static: it is a relative concept and we should avoid the false assumption that just because a person has reached sixty, or seventy, or even eighty, that he cannot change or learn.

3

Assessment — individual aspects of ageing

Before he can reach an understanding of the nature of problems and the necessary treatment the social worker must collect basic data. The formulation of objectives, in other words, requires information. This information will be valuable in so far as it fulfils two conditions: (a) it must be relevant to the recognition of the basic problem in the current situation; (b) it must be relevant to the solution of the problem.

In working with the elderly it is important to bear in mind that almost all problems are multisymptomatic: social, emotional, psychiatric, and medical factors become inextricably linked. Incontinence, for example, may have its basis in physical factors (perhaps an increasing weakness results in stress incontinence), social factors (long garden paths, cold lavatory seats, etc.), or emotional factors (unhappiness, or frustration). In turn the incontinence may cause further social or emotional difficulties in terms of uncleanliness, family stress, or social rejection. Similarly a stroke, with associated chronic disablement, will cause problems of social functioning, with the possibility of affective disorder. It becomes essential, therefore, that working with the elderly should involve working in a team situation: doctors, health visitors, district nurses, and social workers all participate in making a total assessment of the older person's needs.

The social work assessment is carried out with two fundamental objectives. In the first place the assessment is aimed at reaching a decision about the nature of the situation and formulating plans for intervention. In the second place, in his role as team member, the social worker makes a contribution to the team evaluation of the old person and the situation. This contribution will consist, in part, of information about family background, home circumstances and social interaction. There is no skill in the collection of factual knowledge about, for example, the type of housing an old person has, how much his income is, or how many children he has. This is certainly relevant information but in a team context the social worker's task is rather the interpretation of the information in terms of the individual's social functioning. In a social work report the following information is useful and relevant but secondary to the main task:

> Miss A maintains her home well with assistance from a home help twice a week. Her brother visits her regularly and does shopping for her if she is not well enough to go out.

The following extract refers to a hospital patient's functioning in her environment and to the implications of her ageing and disability—very central to the social worker's relationship with her:

> Mrs B is finding it extremely frustrating to adjust to her incapacity. Her independent former existence, coupled with her artistic ability, make it very difficult to accept a change from the role of independent housewife to that of semi-invalid. During our interview she constantly referred to her impairment by word and gesture and indicated considerable determination to do everything in her power to overcome it.

In short, the social worker makes an assessment in order to plan for treatment. In working with the elderly he must be prepared to take information from other professionals as well as contribute to a team plan in return. That contribution consists not so much of social information (although this is a part of the task) but rather an understanding of what that social information means to the particular individual.

Assessment of problems presupposes an ability to identify a non-problematic condition (normality?) as well as a knowledge of problem states, although the actual choice of facts will depend on the state of professional knowledge and on professional choice. In order to discuss some of the ways in which the ageing process affects individuals it is necessary to review them under separate headings. As already pointed out this is a very false division, and developments are usually interdependent aspects of each individual's situation. To make these divisions only serves to emphasise this point.

AGEING AND MENTAL CHANGE

Incidence

Intellectual functioning reaches a peak in the early to middle twenties with a subsequent decline. The rates of decline vary individually but older people are generally slower, more forgetful, less flexible, and tend to prefer routine patterns of life. Environment and physical illness will play a large part in determining the rate of decline of mental abilities and the onset of mental disorder. It has been proposed by some studies that up to a third of old people living in the community are suffering from psychiatric disorder to some extent (Roth and Kay, 1962).

There is evidence that the amount of mental illness is increasing (Agate, 1970) but it is hard to offer definite data because of the difficulties of classifying mental disease in the elderly. Psychoneuroses are frequently suggested as being conditions rarely found in older people but one study (Roth and Kay, 1962), at least, has found a high proportion of people with psychoneurosis severe enough to impair adequate functioning in the community.

The variety of classifications of mental disorders of the elderly is wide: four main groups may be identified: (1) toxic and acute confusional states; (2) affective disorders; (3) chronic brain failure; and (4) late paraphrenia.

Toxic and acute confusional states These are associated with physical conditions. Restlessness, sleeplessness, clouding of consciousness and disorientation characterise behaviour, often with hallucination or delusion, and irrationality, noisiness, and unconnected demands. Delirious confusional behaviour is usually found in feverish illness: illness such as pneumonia, or chronic bronchitis, chronic kidney disease, or an acute cardiovascular episode may also be associated with acute confusion. Drug-induced toxic conditions may also be associated with confused behaviour. Treatment of the cause of the delirium will usually alleviate the confusion and social work intervention may have little to offer the old person. Nevertheless stress on relatives and friends who have to provide care for the old person in these circumstances is considerable and there may be a social work role in helping families to cope with the illness.

Affective disorders Depression is experienced very commonly by old people living at home. In Goldberg's study (1970) of social work and elderly clients about one-third of the elderly people visited experienced very little, but around 20 per cent experienced frequent and prolonged depression. Out of the total sample of 300 people only fifty-five were recorded as showing no depression.

In the elderly, depression may be reactive: it may be due to bereavement, loneliness, or other external factors. More commonly it is endogenous: it has no marked externally precipitating factors and is probably a biochemical disorder. Anxiety and depression can cause extreme suffering for the elderly and it may often be very difficult to identify them as affective disorders, particularly as there may often be an underlying degree of dementia.

Post (1965) has identified several sub-types of depression—organic depression, depressive pseudo-dementia, senile melancholia, agitated depressions, reactive depressions, neurotic depressions, and masked depressions—as well as manic disorders. In doing so he demonstrates the complexity of diagnosis and treatment. If depression has a direct link with external stress, such as bereavement, or perhaps physical illness, the social worker may be in a position to offer therapeutic help. However, the removal of the stress rarely results in the immediate removal of the depression.

Suicidal threats and suicide are a very real part of depression in the elderly: suicide rates in both sexes increase in direct relation to age (Sainsbury, 1962). It is always difficult to distinguish between the threat and the real attempt at suicide but one study demonstrated that general practitioners, when asked if they would tell an old person he was suffering from terminal illness, almost all insisted they would not give the information. Experience had suggested the danger of suicide attempts (Cartwright *et al.*, 1973).

Chronic brain failure Senile dementia is a loose, and sometimes carelessly used term referring to chronic changes in brain function. It is sometimes linked with arteriosclerotic dementia.

(a) *Senile dementia*: a complete disorganisation of behaviour is typical of the later stages of dementia. It is characterised by a slow, and gradual onset, beginning with loss of memory and concentration, a reduction of physical energy, and a mood of shallow depression. Sometimes paranoid ideas and delusions occur, with a general blunting of the emotions and deterioration of intellectual capacities. Finally, anti-social behaviour, incontinence, vagueness, incoherence, wandering and a flat, apathetic mood are evident.

Senile dementia is a non-specific term and causation is not fully understood. Atrophy of the cortical tissue, thickening of the cerebral arteries, and a diffuse loss of nerve cells are common. The distinction between the process of normal ageing and senile dementia lies in the speed with which the changes of senile dementia take place.

(b) *Arteriosclerotic dementia*: dementia may result from a sudden cerebrovascular accident or from more gradual changes. The slower development of arteriosclerotic psychosis fluctuates in severity and there may be sufficient personality preservation for an effort to be made, for a while, to overcome changes. More common in men than women, arteriosclerotic dementia presents changes similar to those of senile dementia but differs in its patchy, irregular progress and in the amount of personality preservation.

(c) *Pre-senile dementia*: dementia in middle-age may arise as a secondary consequence of several disorders, sometimes from injury, or as a result of toxic states. Other conditions have been called 'pre-senile dementia': one such condition, Alzheimer's disease, has recently been more closely associated with the brain changes of senile dementia.

Late paraphrenia   Late paraphrenia is difficult to distinguish from other categories and is often said to include cases of schizophrenia (Agate, 1970) or 'schizophrenia of late onset' (Bromley, 1966). Elderly people with this psychosis develop paranoid delusions. Often linked with hallucinatory experiences, this usually leads to isolation, eccentric behaviour, and withdrawal from common social situations. Paraphrenia is frequently associated with deafness and in spite of common delusions of being controlled, or spied upon, those who suffer from it can remain physically healthy and active for many years.

Attitudes and mental illness

As with other changes that occur in the lives of older people there is a common tendency to assume that psychiatric changes have taken place because of ageing. This is not necessarily so and care must be taken to disentangle the real causes of behaviour change. With our current state of knowledge there seems to be little that social work skills can offer in cases of chronic brain failure—except, perhaps, reassurance and support during the early stages. However, it may be that changes in the life of an individual have reduced his sense of self to such an extent that, for instance, life-long personality aspects which had previously caused no difficulties become major problems. In these circumstances the social worker, by making a careful assessment and subsequent intervention, may be able to relieve external pressures and build up personal strengths to restore more satisfactory functioning.

In the family situation psychiatric change will have varying effects. Increasing rigidity, or lack of flexibility, is a feature of normal ageing: in association with psychiatric illness it may cause considerable difficulty. The old man whose intellectual preservation is insufficient to enable him to perceive the real difficulties of living alone, but who clings determinedly to his independence, often

29

creates great distress for his family, and problems for social work agencies.

Similarly, paranoid ideas and feelings will make it very difficult to provide care for an old person. Often an attempt to make sense of a disordered world will result in the pieces of the jigsaw being put together in the wrong order. The old lady who hides her purse and then forgets where she has put it and then blames the neighbour or home help for stealing it will soon antagonise those who care for her. It is the paranoid ideas and accusations that cause some of the most extreme difficulties in caring for the mentally ill old person in the community. Confused, or forgetful and wandering behaviour will also cause problems: the old lady who gets up in the middle of the night to get a drink and then forgets where she is going and wanders off outside in her nightdress soon starts the family thinking about institutional care.

The importance of mental disease and change for this discussion, then, lies in the effect it has on those who are caring for the old person—who can be helped and supported—rather than its effect on the old person himself—although a lot of work can be done with reactive depression. It is interesting, also, to wonder how effective a programme of social work treatment on patients with a diagnosis of 'senile dementia' might be. Michael Meacher (1972) has suggested that behaving in a confused way may be influenced strongly by being treated as a confused person. Perhaps acquiring a label of 'demented old person' is self-reinforcing.

One final point: the attitudes of the old people who are suffering from mental disorders are hard to comment on—few people have bothered to ask them how they feel about it.

HEALTH AND PHYSICAL CHANGE

Needs and non-reporting

The concept of total health involves much more than just the absence of active disease (Skelton, 1973). It is concerned with the interaction of physical, social and emotional factors and with the sense of well-being associated with a feeling of security. The lack of good health or the need for health-care is very difficult to identify. Most old people say that they are in good health for their age. Several studies (Williamson et al., 1964; Williams et al., 1973; Shanas et al., 1968) of groups of old people have found up to 75 per cent with at least one unknown, moderate, or severe disability. There seems to be no clear relationship between growing older and the likelihood of complaining of poor health, although a relationship has been found between self-evaluation of poor health and real incapacity (Shanas *et al.*, 1968). Older people tend not to complain of illness unless there is a very real physical basis causing, particularly, difficulties of mobility, and it is hard to discuss their 'need' for health services. It is worth noting that the cross-national study by Shanas *et al.* (1968) suggested that national and class factors play some part. Older people in Britain, for example, put a more optimistic interpretation on their impairments and incapacities than do the elderly in Denmark or the USA (and the majority of old people in Britain report that their health is better than the health of other older people). This study also suggested that more 'white-collar' old people had spent part of a previous period in hospital than had elderly people who had formerly been in 'blue-collar' occupations.

Bearing in mind the large proportion of unreported disability there are some general trends in the health of the elderly. A high degree of deficiency, disability and disease does exist among the elderly; some of the pathology may be irremediable but a considerable proportion can be relieved. The control of many diseases (small pox, diphtheria, meningitis, T.B., diabetes, etc.) has increased life expectancy and more people are living to suffer from chronic disease and disability. Sensory loss is common, especially failing sight and deafness: heart disease, arterial disease and hypertension cause problems for many people, as do arthritis and rheumatism. Cancer, too, presents a serious problem. Acute illness does occur in the elderly but need not necessarily be associated with the ageing process. The problem for the geriatrician is the problem in which disease, illness, and disability is connected with factors in the ageing process—psychiatric, emotional and social, as well as physical.

We are concerned here not so much with the aetiology and clinical description of disease or disability among old people as with how illness and physical change affects the elderly individual and how his family react.

Self-esteem and the self-concept

Almost all older people will be involved in a reappraisal of their concept of the physical self. We all carry with us a concept of who we are, and of who we would like to be: this will involve an understanding of what we are physically capable of doing and of what we are incapable of doing. This understanding may be on several levels. On a social level we are each continually presenting a series of social 'faces' or 'impersonations' to the outside world which are designed to convince others around us that we are the sort of person we would like, ideally, to be. Although on a more private, conscious level there may be some inkling of the inconsistencies between the ideal self and the real self, this knowledge is often pushed away to less readily available levels. For some people physical strength, or beauty, may play a large part in their self-concept and for these people physical change may cause particular difficulties, and failure to adjust may involve a painful loss of self-esteem.

For most people the process of readjustment to physical change will be gradual and continuous. For others a sudden physical change, such as that resulting from a stroke, will demand a very rapid reappraisal of the self-concept and a period of grieving for the loss of part of the self may have to take place. During the second meeting of a patients' group in a long-stay geriatric hospital one old lady (who had not attended the first meeting) was asked what she felt about a proposal to establish a social club in the hospital as she had not yet spoken : she responded :

'I wouldn't know about that : I've never been one for mixing socially, and I've never been a drinker. I used to teach music you know, and all I live for is playing the piano.'

Lifting her arthritic fingers she added wistfully :

'I haven't played for a long time though—but now we've got a piano and some music I might be able to try. I couldn't join a club like that : I'm a very musical person and all I want is my piano.'

In setting herself apart in this way she was, to some extent, demonstrating her past behaviour patterns of holding herself aloof from others through her musical ability. In spite of obvious physical obstacles to continuing to play the piano she still clung to this way of behaving towards others and had only partly accepted the reality of the physical change.

Frustration, anxiety and dependence

Closely linked to the threat to self-esteem through physical change are anxieties about practical problems of growing incapacity, as well as the need for information about the future. Frustration may increase and this in turn may be linked with the shifts of dependence which take place as the older person finds he must rely more and more on others. It will be frustrating to have to rely on others to empty commodes (or indeed to have to use a commode), to be unable to light fires, to cook or to do shopping. At any age we experience the conflict between the need to feel both physically secure and cared for, and at the same time the need to remain a separate and individual whole person. The older person will experience this kind of conflict as his physical capacities decline and he finds he relies much more on others; it may be that those who provide most care will become the focus for the frustrated feelings related to this ambivalence. The way the elderly person reacts to the conflict rests, as has already been discussed, very much on the kinds of dependency-needs he has acquired in earlier life.

For some people who need a dependable other person, illness provides a socially acceptable way of achieving that goal. In the sick-role they see nurses, doctors, and other caring people as people to be obeyed with gratitude and once in hospital they may have little incentive to get better because their dependency-needs are being satisfied. Indeed the concern of caring staff tends to lead them to encourage and reward this kind of behaviour as being 'good'. For others, illness and physical change threaten to deprive them of their independence and personal integrity and they will vigorously fight attempts to care for them. One blind and incapacitated old man in an old people's home consistently and determinedly smoked in his bedroom and stubbed out his cigarettes in the wash-basin. Both these activities were expressly forbidden by the matron but by continuing this battle he was able to retain his self-respect and retain an interest in life for a long time.

Family reactions

The effect on families of physical changes in one elderly member will depend on the role that member has previously played within the family—and on the nature of the change. If a parent has for many years been a firm and dependable family head and has been the person to whom children turned in times of trouble then physical change, especially if sudden, may affect the entire family balance. At one extreme the family may react by the complete rejection of the now ineffective parent:

> Mr C was happily married and working in a skilled occupation with a pleasant home in a rural area. His family was closely knit and although the three children were married and living some miles away they visited regularly. Shortly before his sixtieth birthday he had a stroke and was admitted to hospital. After three months he returned home but was unable to walk and had to rely heavily on his wife. Some weeks later he returned to the geriatric hospital with a chest infection

and after his wife expressed doubts about his return home he was transferred to a long-stay ward. Soon after this he spoke freely to the social worker: a devout Catholic he was particularly worried about events in Africa when he was young which he was unable to describe but which he suggested were evil enough to account for his current 'punishment'. During this period his wife visited daily but on one occasion she said in his presence that it was a pity he had not died in the first place rather than dragging on. After this he gradually became withdrawn, apathetic, and depressed: his head sank on his chest and he answered questions mono-syllabically. His wife and children continued to visit and reinforce by word and action that they would rather have grieved for his death than his ineffectuality. Eventually Mr C was able to die: it was evident that he had set out to achieve his own death because of his family's spoken and unspoken pressures which colluded with his own tendency to self-blame.

Few situations are so extreme. For many families the ageing of the elderly members is a process of gradual adjustment. In middle classes, patterns of help usually continue to be from parents to children; in the working classes, patterns of help tend to take a child to parent direction. This is partly for financial reasons and partly because children of white-collar parents are more likely to move away from home. It is therefore hard to generalise about family reactions: physical change, disease, and disability of one member of the family do present emotional and practical problems for the rest of the family members.

Death

Increasing physical degeneration highlights the approach and inevitability of death. In a study of fear in old age (Papalia *et al.*, 1973) people who expressed no fear were asked to what they attributed this. The responses fell into three categories: preparing for death, good health, and spiritual trust (being God-fearing). Death has to be faced, and acceptance and the necessity for facing it are related to health and physical change.

Incontinence

It is impossible to discuss the emotional implications of physical change in ageing without considering incontinence. Not only does urinary or faecal incontinence have medical, social, and emotional aspects but it is frequently used as an administrative weapon: the incontinent patient is difficult to cope with in his own home but will often be unacceptable for local authority accommodation. Many incontinent older people become held up in the institutional system because they are unsuitable for transfer from hospital to old people's homes: for this reason the problem assumes an exaggerated importance.

Setting aside these problems (as well as the true medical aspects, and laziness, precipitancy, long garden paths and outside lavatories, etc.) it does seem that incontinence may often be used as a way of expressing and communicating unhappiness, or anger. To withhold or produce at the wrong moment gives power: one way to help is to understand the message and create other, less troublesome avenues for self-expression.

Illness and disability—summary

This discussion has not attempted primarily to identify symptoms and causes of disease but has been concerned with how it feels to be inside a physically changing body, and also with how it feels to be a member of the family of an ageing person in terms of his physical changes. For the individual a reconsideration of his concept of physical self seems inevitable: frustration linked to increased dependence on others and a prompting of thoughts about death are also possible reactions. In the family situation a readjustment of dependence may take place but reactions will vary because of the vast range of class, cultural, and personality factors involved.

SOCIAL ASPECTS OF AGEING

In a sense any problem experienced by an ageing person is a social problem: it is difficult to draw limits on the discussion but some general problem areas will be considered.

Occupational changes

Work means different things to different people and the meanings will vary from class to class and will also depend on the nature of the occupation. Work is usually proposed, in industrial societies, as being primarily an economic necessity. Attitudes to retirement will also vary according to attitudes to work as well as more general approaches to life, and similarly leisure (or an increased amount of free time) will be differently used.

Retirement and roles   People tend to define themselves in terms

of their occupation, or former occupation: bus driver, teacher, mechanic, etc. Retirement from active participation in the work situation will involve a loss of many of the roles associated with occupation: wage-earner, employee, employer, etc. In addition it will involve the loss of many other roles linked indirectly with work: retiring workers stop being people who use the 8 o'clock train or go to the pub round the corner from work at lunch time, etc. These losses will require adjustment in various ways. Within the family group a change in the male status from being bread-winner to being 'under foot' in the house during the day may cause stress. Similarly, difficulties may arise in a family in which communication has generally been channelled from the mother directly to the children, or from the father to the children through the mother. In this situation new patterns of communication may have to be established with greater or lesser success.

Retirement and disengagement   Returning for a while to disengagement, some studies (Crawford, 1972; Shanas *et al.*, 1968) have looked at the relationship of disengagement and retirement. Crawford identified four groups of reactions to anticipated retirement, differentiated by sex and social class. She found, first, a group of men who looked forward to retirement because they were involved in a number of roles outside their work situation and they saw retirement as providing an opportunity to become more involved in these outside activities. They tended to be non-manual workers and saw the retirement period in terms of freedom and leisure. A second group of men, mainly in manual occupations, depended heavily on their work situation for satisfactions. They saw retirement as a period of isolation and removal from their earlier ways of achieving satisfaction and tended to concentrate on the losses rather than the constructiveness of the situation. Third, a group of women, largely the wives of non-manual workers, found their satisfactions in the home and looked forward to retirement as a time to draw their husbands more fully into the family situation. Finally, a group of women were found to be involved in activities outside the home. They dreaded retirement because they had re-adjusted their lives after the children left home and feared being tied to the home again. They were mainly married to manual workers.

The conclusion would obviously be that manual workers and their wives fear retirement while non-manual workers and their families look forward to it. The former face enforced disengagement and the latter a satisfying re-engagement. In fact the position is not nearly so clear cut and attitudes and reactions shade into each other but it is important to recognise that social environment has a bearing on these attitudes. As Shanas *et al.* have said (1971), there is no evidence that disengagement is a necessary concomitant of retirement for all or even most workers; and actual enjoyment of the post-retirement period may differ radically from previously anticipated enjoyment.

Enjoyment: retirement and leisure The reasons for retirement may play a part in adjustment and enjoyment. The cross-national study of Shanas *et al.* (1968) suggested that stated reasons for retirement may include an attempt at justification. For example, if, in a particular social group, it is considered unacceptable not to work, then more 'acceptable' reasons may be used such as ill-health. In other situations high unemployment may lead to reasons such as 'able to afford to retire'. In the study, it was found that bad health or reasons linked to physical change were most commonly presented, with compulsory retirement and redundancy also figuring largely. Men who were already in retirement were more likely to claim that their retirement was by choice rather than as a result of arbitrary imposition.

In general this study found that men in Britain saw the retirement period as a time to rest from a lifetime of labouring (in contrast to the USA where it was seen as a time to enjoy all the things that work had prevented them from doing). Men who have retired do not say they miss anything from work but they do miss income: at a time when their needs are changing they lack the money to pay for the resources to meet these changing needs. Continuing good health also has an effect: the less he enjoys good health the more likely a man is to view past work with nostalgia. The cross-national study does conclude that there seems to be a cut-off point after which people seem to accept their roles as a retired person: the longer the retirement period the less likely they are to miss anything about work.

As long as the majority of retired people have an inadequate income it seems unlikely that retirement will be widely viewed as a period of complete satisfaction. The preface to the report of the Third International Course of Social Gerontology (1972) begins:

The third age is the age of leisure.
That is to say:
> the age of choice
> of preferential orientation
> of freedom

None of these is possible without adequate income but other

barriers to the perception of retirement as a time of leisure and freedom exist as well.

Leisure means having time at one's own disposal. It is a concept that can be viewed in many terms—the humanistic, as an end in itself; the therapeutic, as a means of control; the quantitative, as time left over after work is finished; the institutional, as distinct from such behaviours as political, educational, religious, etc.; and the epistemological, as relating activities and meanings to the assumptive, analytical and aesthetic views of the world (Kaplan, 1972). Leisure is concerned with time, with freedom and with satisfaction, and all these factors rest on social, cultural, and environmental factors and attitudes.

Play for the child fulfils a number of functions: exploration and movement, make-believe, imitation and preparation for future roles, learning, and expression of feelings. In a similar way play may fulfil the needs of older people. It may provide a socially accepted expression for feelings and energies; it may provide an opportunity for the displacement and acting out of needs and feelings which cannot be otherwise expressed. Opportunities for play may also allow the retired person to explore and experiment with new roles: facing difficulties and conflicts in situations of play gives each person the chance to grow and develop through the resolution of conflict. If leisure and play can be continued, growth and satisfaction will be associated with them. Using leisure, however, involves not only having sufficient income, time, and facilities for each individual to participate in activities of his choice but it also requires changing attitudes to the retirement period.

Pre-retirement and retirement education Preparation for retirement cannot begin too soon. Occupational pensions, in particular, must be planned and organised early in life and other financial plans should also be laid as early as possible. Most pre-retirement education in this country is run on the basis of a short course of lectures and discussions held six months, or up to a year or two, before retirement. The courses cover such subjects as physical health, finance, housing, income tax, and leisure activities. Long-term assessment of the value and effects of pre-retirement education is rare and difficult. Course participants may be stimulated to think about retirement problems, but this is, in any case, a part of the motivation for (voluntary) attendance on courses. The most definite reaction tends to be to health information, and to a slightly less positive extent, to financial information.

A further consideration is the provision of a wide range of adult education facilities for the retired. A large proportion of those attending adult education classes are people who have retired.

Move to retirement areas Retirement resorts are phenomena of industrialised society. The United States have had their 'retirement cities' for a long time—Palm Springs, Carmel, etc. Britain is now showing a trend of migration to retirement areas, especially near the sea: the south coast shows the trend vividly, particularly the Brighton and Bournemouth areas. This trend has a number of implications. Severing of family ties and social support networks may not be a major problem for those who retain their health and strength and can make the return journey to their previous homes, and can become involved in the new community. Others may find that failing strength or the death of a spouse cause withdrawal from the world but without an available support network. In these areas with a high proportion of older people problems arise not only of who will staff the social services but of who will pay for them. Incomes in the resorts are low, work is seasonal and is largely in retail and catering jobs which are relatively low-paid. In comparison to the national average, incomes in the resorts tend to be low and money to meet the increased demand for social services is lacking.

Uprooting after retirement and moving to the sea may bring short-term satisfactions but tends to cause major long-term problems.

Retirement and loss For all people retirement means loss. Most will adjust to this loss gradually and do so in terms of coping mechanisms learned in earlier-life situations. Others will actively enjoy the retirement period and will find new satisfactions to replace what they have lost and extend their lives in new directions —in spite of limited opportunities to do this in this country. For a small minority retirement will present a loss situation with which they are unable to deal through normal coping mechanisms. A failure of adjustment may follow unsuccessful grieving for the past and chronic maladaptive behaviour results. It is worth remembering that retirement may be one cause of difficulties in ageing, and later problems and dissatisfactions may be rooted partly in failure to have adjusted to retirement.

LIVING ALONE AND LONELINESS

Living alone does not necessarily cause loneliness. Many people who live alone have chosen to do so and many others do not feel lonely.

Who lives alone? Living alone is on the increase. Of the total households in Great Britain in 1951, 10·7 per cent were people living alone; in 1966 this proportion had risen to 15·4 per cent. Older people are more likely than others to live alone: in 1966 some 65·4 per cent of all single-person households were of people over pensionable age. In any one region the proportion of old people living alone is largely dependent on a range of social and economic factors of which the nature, quality and supply of hous- ing is probably the most important (Tunstall, 1966). A childless person has an increased chance of living alone: Tunstall suggested the old person without children has as much as twice the chance of living alone as the person with a child living. The chances of living alone in old age seem to depend more on numbers of children living, and marital status, than on socio-economic variables.

Living alone and isolation Few people live in extreme isolation from others, in the sense of lacking significant interaction with other people (Shanas *et al.*, 1968). Isolation in relationship terms may be from primary or secondary groups. In the sense of isolation from the wider community groups, and opportunities for social interaction, measures of isolation demonstrate a significant con- nection between living alone and social isolation. Tunstall's study found 65 per cent of men and 69 per cent of old women living alone could be categorised as socially isolated on the basis of less than twenty contacts (of a more than 'casual' nature) during the week previous to interview.

Isolation, in the sense of having few contacts with other people, is closely linked to living alone. People who continue to work, or who have at least one child alive, are less likely to be isolated. People who are isolated tend to be older, single, or widowed, without children and close family, retired, and infirm. Isolation tends to be a function of the interaction of three or more of these aspects (Shanas *et al.*, 1968). Obviously, isolation is linked to certain deprivations and it is in turn connected with the likelihood of people saying they are lonely.

Loneliness involves lack of companionship and has taken on additional implications of unhappiness or dissatisfaction. It has been defined as the condition of an individual who desires contact with others but is unable to achieve it (Women's Group on Public Welfare, 1957). It is associated with deprivation and with isolation. Only a minority of older people say they are often or sometimes lonely (28 per cent in Britain—Shanas *et al.*, 1968): isolation, as such, seems not to account for feeling lonely but deprivation, particularly through bereavement, may be a cause. However, those old people who experience bereavement are less likely to complain of loneliness if they are able to build up and extend substitute relationships.

Implications for practice Living alone is a problem of the elderly as a group, in contrast to younger age groups. Living alone has been found to predispose to isolation which in turn may predispose to loneliness. Aloneness and loneliness tend not to show social class differentials and seem to depend more on the lack of, or more especially on deprivation of, relationships—particularly with children, or husbands and wives—than on socio-economic variables.

The old person who is unhappy, perhaps initially because of bereavement, will have little inclination to seek social contacts: the more rejecting he is of help the less help will be offered. A self-reinforcing process of apathy/antipathy may develop which at its worst is only halted by a crisis of illness or social collapse.

In less extreme situations the social worker can help the old person to cope with the pressures which cause unhappiness or loneliness, help to provide substitute relationships and prevent the vicious circle in which loneliness and desolation become their own reinforcers. It is important not to lose sight of the fact that some people choose to live alone. Being alone therefore is not a justification, in itself, for the assumption that loneliness exists, and the consequent imposition of help.

AGEING AND THE FAMILY

As has already been emphasised most old people do receive support from their families, if they need it and do retain continuing contact. The majority of elderly people in fact do live either alone or with only the marriage partner but of those who have children and live apart from them well over three-quarters see at least one child regularly and frequently. The nature and extent of this contact in terms of help given or received depends on both the sex and age of the parent or social class variables.

Shanas *et al.* (1968) found a number of similar changes in patterns in family relationships with ageing in Britain, Denmark and the USA: (1) more old people live with children, both unmarried and married; (2) more old people live close to children; (3) more old people report recent contacts with children; (4) more old people report help from their children; (5) fewer old people report that they are able to help their children.

The pattern presented is undoubtedly one of increasing dependence, and support from children is usually extended as parents grow older. Practical studies of caring services have demonstrated similar patterns, in more extreme situations (Isaacs, 1972). Families will usually continue to accept an obligation to care for ageing parents and will often only allow ill old people to be admitted to hospital care when they have reached the limit of endurance. This determination of many families to provide care for as long as possible is one of the causes of conflict so often apparent in working with the elderly and will be examined in detail later.

Nuclear and extended families Sociological theory has devoted much of its thinking to the concept of the nuclear family. The concept of kinship is fundamental to the idea of the nuclear family : kinship relationships are ascribed on the basis of biological and culturally determined ideas. In addition to this marriage can be described as the creation of relationships between groups as well as individuals and a rearrangement of the relationships between people (C. C. Harris, 1969). The nuclear family is, then, a group of people carrying out a number of interrelated activities which define and are in turn defined by its membership. The family in this sense carries out social functions: reproduction, socialisation, protection, support, etc. A good deal of work has been done on these functions in relation to the children within the family and to marital roles. A much more limited approach to the problems of the elderly person in relation to his family has been centred on discussion of the extended family. Most of the work on family roles and interactions, however, has tended to stop with a consideration of middle-age and adjustment to the transition when the children develop their own family nucleus.

Development and the life-cycle An approach which has taken the problem a little further is that which presents the family as coping with a number of different developmental tasks at any one point in time, each task being different but all interrelated. Marriage, reproduction and death are all interdependent and all may be occurring at the same time, even though they may represent opposing trends. In this sense development occurs through a cyclical process of never-ending tasks: a generation spiral exists whereby death may remove one family member but not the totality of that member's influence on the development that is yet to come. The relevance of what has already happened in the family is at least as important as the relevance of what has yet to come.

It may, on the other hand, be suggested that this is not a cyclical process but a collection, or joining together of several individuals each performing tasks appropriate to his own stage of development. Whatever the basis it does seem that many families are actively involved in providing care for elderly parents, or other older relatives. What, then, are some of the factors involved in the family interaction?

Dependence and the family Most people as they grow older will experience and play several roles within the family—child, parent, mother or father, grandparent, husband, wife, etc. Dependence can never be an entirely submissive experience and the ability to affect the balance of power in any relationship can exist on both sides: ostensibly the young baby is dependent on his parents for his physical needs but that does not prevent him from exerting a considerable influence on them through his demands. In a healthy sense dependence produces growth; in a pathological sense it may be used to provide neurotic satisfactions. In order to see the influence of this on family roles three aspects of family development will be examined: parenthood and the growth of children from the family group; grandparenthood; and marriage.

As children grow up in the family various changes and adjustments have to be made. Sexual development in the child may result in his being treated as a dangerous (as a threat to the father, for example) or endangered object (over-protection). Sometimes the child who reaches early adulthood may be an object of envy to a parent and sometimes the parents may find it difficult to 'let go' of him as he moves into an independent life. Ageing of the family itself, therefore, usually means a breaking up of the family in some of its functioning. Children are now being launched into the world when their parents are younger than in earlier generations. This leads to a longer period during which the mother and father live alone together and this in itself may lead to strain.

Bearing in mind the social class variations in patterns of help from parent to child, or vice versa, as parents age there is an increased chance that they will become physically, financially, or emotionally dependent on children. This may occur while the gradual ageing process reduces abilities and most people do not become physically dependent on children until relatively late in life. For others a sudden physical change such as that following a stroke, or the less sudden but equally incapacitating effects of Parkinsonism, or osteo-arthritis, may cause a sudden reappraisal of the family position. From being the respected, dependable head of the family, to whom other members look for support, advice and guidance, an ageing person may become physically dependent and reliant on child or spouse for very basic help. Particularly where this is a sudden occurrence the family may be unable to cope without help:

Mr D ran a small farm with the help of his wife and family. In his early 60s he had a stroke but was making a reasonably good physical recovery. The social worker visited in connection with Mr D's attendance at a day hospital and several visits were made to the farm during which the interviews were conducted on a very practical level:

'I was invited in for coffee and talked at length about the client's problems. These are focused on his visual impairment which prevents him taking much of an active part in running the farm: he also has great difficulty in mental co-ordination regarding figures (i.e. his book-keeping) and finds great difficulty in reading. He did not present as being unduly worried about this but I believe he was hiding underlying anxiety. His wife has become well adjusted to her husband's incapacity but finds the farm work heavy going despite help from her sons.'

Mr and Mrs D persisted in presenting this picture during another interview two weeks later. A further two weeks later they were seen again and after talking to Mr D who insisted he was quite capable of coping with all the farm work the social worker reported:

'When a friend came to see him I took the opportunity to see his wife alone. She immediately launched into a distressed narrative about the client and his behaviour. I was given to understand Mr D actually did very little about the farm but refused offers of help that were badly needed. He has become suspicious about money, aggressive over minor things and there had been a profound deterioration in marital relations. Mrs D cried quite bitterly and is under severe emotional strain aggravated by the heavy physical demands that the farm work is placing on her ... the relationship is now in a crucial phase ... his wife can only relate to him in terms of their former lives. The loss of physical contact and open demonstrations of love hurt her more than anything else.'

In this kind of situation there has to be a grieving for the former relationship and the former physical self before growth to a new understanding can proceed. As the children grow away from the parental family they begin to develop their own families and so affect status even further. Becoming a grandparent may cause a crisis of self-perception in forcing the grandmother or grandfather to recognise their age: in compensation it offers an additional status. Grandparenthood brings an aura of maturity and status among peers and it also brings the opportunity to enjoy relationships with the children without responsibility and excess physical effort.

Dependence exists in all relationship situations and may be exaggerated and become the basis for neurotic satisfactions in a few ageing people. If the baby can be the most powerful person in the house then so can the frail, dependent elderly parent who may act out infantile needs that have been under control for most of his life.

Marriage As people live longer so it becomes more likely that married couples will survive together for longer. It has already been suggested that as children also leave home earlier the years together as a couple are even more extended. These extra years may be seen as a time to share and enjoy, together, all the things that couldn't be done while the children were at home. Alternatively, the strain of living continually in companionship all day long may be too much for the relationship: some marriages thrive on the daily separations caused by working-routines but cannot stand up to enforced proximity. The fact that a marriage has continued for thirty years is no guarantee of its future survival.

Having negotiated the 'flight from the nest' of the children a further hurdle to be overcome is that of retirement. If the husband is worried and concerned about the approach of retirement, while his wife feels little involvement it will not be possible for them to plan effectively for adjustment. If the husband does find it difficult to make an adjustment then the wife will be drawn into the difficulties whether she had previously felt herself involved or not. On the whole, husbands tend to have more expectations of retirement and show a greater sense of improvement and satisfaction in retirement than their wives (Kerckhoff, 1964).

The continuance of sexual behaviour in marriage is dependent mainly on habit: if sexual intercourse is continued regularly there is no physiological reason why it should not be enjoyed into old age. The likelihood of continuing sexual relationships may also be influenced by the attitudes of others outside the marriage. If the children are shocked or react negatively to the knowledge of continuing relationships this may have an inhibiting effect. The attitudes of doctors may also have an important influence: a surprised reaction from a general practitioner may confirm suspicions

45

already held about the physical advisability of sexual intercourse in old age.

Widowhood produces significant changes in interpersonal relationships. Not only are widowed people much more vulnerable to ill-health and even death (especially widowed old men) but they tend not to fit in with married couples who had been friends. Unless the widowed person can find an acceptable partner, social interaction outside the family becomes difficult because the number of social activities for single people is limited.

The single, ageing adult Those who have not been married are normally deprived of the support of children and it is apparent that those who lack this support are most vulnerable to the problems of ageing (although having children is no guarantee of a satisfactory old age and may even create problems). Perhaps this is more significant for women than for men, who are able to build up satisfactions in the work situation and can look back on work as a time of creativity. There are situations in which single people can use their creative energies in socially acceptable ways which can continue into old age, but in general being single, like being widowed, means vulnerability to social, emotional and economic deprivation as well as ill-health.

Psychoanalysis and the ageing family Only limited attention has been given by psychoanalytical thinking to relationships between ageing parents and their middle-aged children. It is tempting to think about 'oedipus fifty years on' and transpose triangular conflicts of early life into later-life situations. There is no doubt that father-son conflicts continue through life in varying forms and may be heightened when the father finds himself, at sixty-five, with obsolete skills and a low market-value at a time when his son is at the peak of his career and achievement. There are undoubtedly daughters who, having got their increasingly frail and elderly mothers at their mercy, take a neurotic delight in getting revenge for a lifetime of intimidation or suppression. To discuss these kinds of situation, though they are not uncommon, is to discuss essentially fixated or regressive behaviour.

An alternative that has been suggested (Blenkner, 1965) is the addition of a stage of 'filial maturity' to the process of development. The filial crisis occurs in most people when they are in their forties and fifties: this crisis involves seeing the parents as less dependable and beginning to need support from the child. The resolution of this crisis consists in taking on the filial task—being dependable—and the subsequent achievement of filial maturity. In this view the role-reversal view of the child becoming 'father to his father' following physical change in the parent is a pathological approach. Taking on the filial role and achieving filial maturity is a normal and inevitable part of family life and the healthy resolution of the filial crisis means leaving behind the rebellion of adolescence and turning once more to the parent, but this time as a mature adult.

If this view is accepted, and the task of the middle-aged child is achieving a mature dependability, then there is an important role for the social worker. To help the middle-aged client to accept the needs and demands of his ageing parent will be to help him to grow into a new maturity. A preventive social work approach must include this view: although most families do cope with their elderly members perfectly adequately (unless physical circumstances prevent it), a few are unable to negotiate the filial crisis.

Scapegoating One common, neurotic family reaction to dependency-changes of an elderly parent is the need to scapegoat. Often identified and described in connection with children in families and individuals in group situations, scapegoating may also be a reaction to old people. Scapegoating, as far as the family is concerned, serves the functional purpose of preserving solidarity and strength among the majority of members. By identifying one person as the holder of all the badness in the situation, the others can preserve their own selves through mutual support and overcome the existence of conflict in other areas of family functioning. For the old person who is scapegoated extreme unhappiness, loneliness, isolation, and depression may result. He may over-react by colluding with the family's view of himself and become very bad—very irritable, confused, incontinent, demanding, dominating, etc. Here again is an important task for the social worker in reducing the pressure on the old person by helping the family examine the real situation and by clarifying for the old person the meaning of his own and his family's behaviour.

LOSS AND BEREAVEMENT

It should be plain by now that ageing presents the individual with a number of loss situations each of which has to be overcome and compensated for in some way. Ageing represents shrinkage but for most people this can provide satisfactions, and losses are absorbed with the support of the family and friends.

Bereavement As people grow older they are more likely to experience bereavement as their friends, peers, husbands or wives grow older alongside them and are more at risk. However well prepared they are for death relatives will be shocked, although it has been suggested (Lamerton, 1973) that the process of adjustment is easier for the elderly, who expect death to come to those who are close to them, than it is, for example, for the young widow or parent of a child.

Reactions to bereavement do seem to follow a 'normal' predictable pattern. In the first few days, a stunned, empty, numbness is felt and the bereaved person finds it hard to believe his loss, and may even deny the death. After this period of emptiness grief as a kind of searching for the lost person begins, but a searching that is constantly frustrated. Periods of intense physical distress, alternating with apathy, disinterest and occasionally anger, are characteristic. Sometimes the anger is directed outwards at a scapegoat—perhaps the doctor who didn't do enough to help, or the social worker who can't understand. Sometimes there may be a feeling of relief, and later guilt, particularly when death follows a long period of illness.

Following a normal pattern the intensity usually begins to die away after about six weeks and does not cause serious problems by about six months after the death. If this pattern is not followed, however, chronic, pathological reactions will be characteristic. Bitterness, anxiety, and guilt may be excessive and occasionally hallucinations of the dead person are described. In these cases social workers can do much to help to release the pent-up feelings which may often have been contained through lack of acceptable social means of expression. It is important that grief is allowed expression, and involvement in planning funeral arrangements with the undertaker is a very important first step in releasing grief.

Bereavement reactions are not, of course, restricted to the loss of a person. The loss of physical strength, or a limb, or the use of part of the body may cause grief reactions in both the individual who suffers the loss as well as his family:

Mr E was 82 when he suffered a cardiovascular accident and he was admitted, after a few weeks delay, to a geriatric assessment ward. The social worker visited the home:

'Mrs E seen at home. She is much younger than her husband by fifteen years. Since his admission to hospital she has reorganised the home to suit her own convenience and has quickly adapted to living on her own.... I gained the impression that Mrs E was just waiting for his death and as far as his home was concerned he was written off.'

By re-arranging the home to look as though her husband

had never existed Mrs E was demonstrating symbolically her feeling of total loss. When arrangements had been made for his return home it was commented during another visit:

'It was noticeable that all necessary arrangements had been made for his return home—his bed, armchair, and other personal belongings had re-appeared ... During this visit Mrs E revealed her own personal difficulties in having to accept the more responsible role in the home: she had always looked to her husband to make decisions, manage the family finances, etc.'

With the return home of Mr E his wife was unable to pretend he was gone for ever and had to face up to her changed responsibilities and need to grieve for the loss of the dependable part of her husband with the social worker.

Similarly, the loss of a home may cause a grief reaction and the dazed, regressive behaviour of people admitted to old people's homes may represent something of this tendency.

Mrs F, a widow of 63, contacted the Social Services Department herself, saying that the doctor had suggested she needed a convalescent holiday:

'The house', reported the social worker, 'is in a chaotic state. The floor is covered with bare lino with only one small rug (although the furniture is of good quality and she says she has a substantial pension) and the surfaces of the furniture are equally bare.

... She told me she had moved from the other side of the city a year ago because she said she had been lonely ... she has no friends or family in this area.

... She didn't mention the holiday but complained at length about the neighbours, the landlord, her health, and the unfriendly people in this area.

... Eventually she blurted out that she wished she'd never left the other house: that was where her husband died, eleven years ago last week.'

Mrs F's grief for her husband, never adequately resolved because of lack of family support, had become muddled with her loss of the last house. This house showed her inner emptiness and unresolved grief in its bareness and chaos.

Dying Lamerton (1973) has described a 'joyful process of dying' whereby, he argues, fears and distress in dying can be reduced by the control of pain. Euthanasia is irrelevant in this argument

49

because in an ideal world pain need not exist. Nevertheless pain does exist in a very real way and up to 70 per cent of dying people have been identified as suffering from pain in some degree in the year prior to death (Cartwright *et al.*, 1973).

In dealing with the dying it is important to distinguish their fear of death from that of those around them. Dying people need others to be with them and fear of death should not prevent those others from giving them the support they need. The social worker may be involved both in supporting the dying and in supporting those who are caring for the dying to help them continue in their support. Many people want to die at home and relatives may feel guilty if they have to send them into hospital for their last few days. Some old people seem to achieve a serene acceptance of death:

> Mrs G was dying of cancer and knew she would die before the weekend:
> 'I know it's right: I'm very tired and I want to go ...
> My son has come from America: I couldn't live with him:
> I couldn't stand the trip. He accepts it too, and we've talked about it—we can call each other Peace ... and the world's in such a mess anyway, everything's war and chaos. I'm very tired.'

Although outwardly calm this lady demonstrates some of her inner uncertainty in talking of the chaotic state of the world—perhaps a projective fantasy.

SUMMARY

The problems then that the individual may meet as he grows older tend to be problems of loss. He may be deprived of roles and status, he may lose friends, family, support, or adequate income and housing. He may also experience changes in mental or physical function.

Ageing involves adjustment to deprivation—for the majority this adjustment is made gradually and new satisfactions are added as some long-term satisfactions are built up and strengthened. A minority will need outside help to ease them over difficulties and may call on the Church, or health and statutory social services as well as voluntary organisations. It is important that any help given is directed not just towards solving a static problem in the here-and-now but that it should aim to restore the interrupted process of ageing to a normal, satisfying progression.

A pattern of successful ageing will be seen to grow out of a recognition of the normality of the process and of the fact that problems are only relevant in terms of this process. In selecting information for assessment the social worker should consider the relevance of the information to the client: does he see it in problem terms: is it an important block to the achievement of a continued life-process: and does it prevent satisfaction?

4

Communication

Communication, like assessment, is by no means the sole prerogative of the social worker. Nevertheless communication is an important part of the process of gathering information, attaching meanings to the information and, also, it is a part of building up relationships and providing practical help.

THE NATURE OF COMMUNICATION

To attempt a definition of communication in social work is to attempt the impossible. Any definition must certainly include the imparting, sharing and transmitting of information but beyond this it involves perception by both the giver of the information and the recipient.

Communication from one person to another will be, at least in part, made up of perceptions put together from non-verbal messages. Messages will be transmitted and picked up on many levels: on a static, physical level, physique, hair colour, nose shape, type of clothing, etc., suggest certain things about people. On a more dynamic, expressive level, movements, facial expression, etc., give indications. Less tangible are the messages implicit in the things that people do, the way they react in situations—in the context of their behaviour rather than the behaviour itself. Assessment of others is therefore based on perception of non-verbal communications, as well as actual spoken information received from the individual or others around him.

It will be plain that when the social worker picks up messages from clients in such a range of unsophisticated ways subjectivity is inevitable. Over-simplification, stereotyping and projection are common dangers. It is all too easy to imagine that because one old person with a particular appearance behaves in a particular way then another with a similar appearance will behave in the same way. It is equally easy to fall into the trap of basing perceptions on stereotypes of old age: all old people are depressed, old people are like children, old people want to live quiet lives, etc. In communicating with the client a social worker receives input from several sources, verbal and non-verbal, and he must continually attempt to achieve a total understanding of the information and of its meaning to the client and to himself.

THE OBJECTIVES OF COMMUNICATION

Why, then, does the social worker need to be able to communicate? The primary objective of good communication is, of course, the achievement of understanding. Before an effective relationship can develop there must be an establishment of basic trust which in turn rests on a degree of mutual knowledge. This does demand a level of communication and the worker must not only be able to receive messages clearly but must also be able to present himself and his objectives in such a way that the client will be able to accept and use the information.

Communication is, therefore, an essential prerequisite to assessment. An appropriate diagnosis cannot be made unless the facts are gathered together and this gathering together will only be possible if those who are a part of the social situation feel free to divulge the information. They must also feel free to express their feelings about the social situation in which they find themselves. Only then will the social worker have enough information to be able to begin to interpret the meaning of the total problem to each individual involved.

From this collection and interpretation of information the worker can begin to formulate plans for future intervention and action, and can communicate these plans to the client. Inevitably this is a process that begins with the initial contact: as soon as he begins to communicate with the client the social worker is also beginning an intervention which becomes part of the treatment relationship. Every message from the worker, received by the client, contributes to the nature of the relationship that is built up.

Communication is not in itself an objective of social work but it is an essential part of the development of assessment and treatment, and as such is part of the task of the social worker. Communication is not just between two people: it may take place between social worker and client groups, colleague groups, and community groups. It will also take place between agencies, through the social worker as the representative of an agency, or within agencies and institutions. In each case the objective of communication for the social worker is the maximisation of understanding and the minimisation of misunderstanding.

COMMUNICATION AND THE ELDERLY CLIENT

On a superficial level there are obvious aspects of communication with the elderly that depend on their actual age. Those who are now in their seventies and eighties have lived through particular common life experiences, notably two world wars and a world depression. On the basis of their having lived through more than the younger person old people may have different perceptions, expectations, and dislikes. These may be based on the common experiences of particular cultural changes that old people have passed through and they may be based on the life experiences of each individual older person. As a result of this communication between older and younger people may be slightly clouded but far less clouded, perhaps, than for the middle-class social worker in a working-class family situation, or for the worker with an immigrant family, etc.

There are much more clear-cut problems in attempting to understand and communicate with old people. Often these are based on physical changes.

Sensory deprivation—the extent The tendency of old people to deny ill-health, or to fail to report it, means that information on the full extent of sensory deprivation is limited. Studies show some general agreement. About a third of elderly people suffer from hearing difficulties and about 6 per cent of the elderly experience such difficulties to a severe extent. Several visual disorders affect about 8 per cent of the elderly while 22 per cent experience some degree of visual impairment (Townsend and Wedderburn, 1965).

Over the age of about forty-five most older people experience some degree of long-sightedness (Agate, 1970), although almost perfect sight may continue throughout a long life. The processes of age-change in vision are usually complex: changes in the retina, fading of the iris, thickening of the cornea, changes in the nervous system may all contribute. The process is further complicated by changes in alertness and attention that occur with ageing.

Hearing-loss is often gradual and may not be noticed for a long time because the sounds which tend to be lost are those which are irrelevant to normal functioning. Eventually many older people experience, in particular, a high-tone hearing-loss but the total picture is blurred because other factors are involved in the ability to hear speech: linguistic ability, concentration, interest, etc., are all part of hearing.

Another loss which may cause communication difficulties is the loss of the ability to speak. Normally the voice tends to become more highly pitched as the person progresses into old age and speech is slower, with more pauses (Bromley, 1966). Pathological speech-changes may result from a variety of disease and disability.

Incapacity increases with age: the most seriously incapacitated old people are those who are over seventy-five or eighty years of age. The likelihood of experiencing impairment sufficiently serious to be a handicap in communicating with others is therefore greater for the very old. Since it is this group that is increasing at a proportionately higher rate it is more and more likely that problems of social workers in communicating with the elderly will become more common.

Sensory deprivation as a barrier to communication In the social work relationship so much of the expression of caring and concern rests on non-verbal actions and behaviour. This goes far beyond the friendly gesture, or the sympathetic smile, but involves the presentation of the worker's whole attitude to the client and his needs and feelings. If the client is blind, or deaf, or even both, much of the impact of the usual non-verbal content of communications will be lost and just spending time with the client, silence and touch take on a greater importance.

The shape and form of interviews with partially deaf clients will need to be reorganised—a good enabling remark designed to help an old lady to pour out her heart tends to lose much of its impact after it has been bellowed in her ear for the sixth time! The content of verbal communication from worker to client has to be more concise, less suggestive and more precise than with younger, physically able clients. In these situations a great deal of patience and determination may be demanded of the worker if he is to hear the client's real message. In structuring an interview the first objective is to create an environment in which the client can feel free to express himself: it must also be an environment in which the worker can receive the message. To reach these objectives the social worker has to be flexible in his use of techniques of communication when working with the older person with sensory loss.

Close relatives and members of nursing staff in long-stay hospitals for old people are often able to understand what patients with speech difficulties are trying to stay. They will understand a request for a cigarette, a sleep, a trip to the lavatory, or comments on the weather. This understanding comes from close, continual contact and is frequently very perceptive; occasionally the message may be misinterpreted and the result is extreme frustration for the patient. Frustration is the central, fundamental problem of sensory deprivation: frustration as an overwhelming sense of impotence and anger directed everywhere at once—internally and externally. The social worker does not have the advantages of the nurse or close relative in learning about the speechless client's real meaning: he must try to understand the whole client from a bare minimum of information and failure to understand appropriately may cause considerable frustration.

In addition chronic brain failure will lead to confusion and forgetfulness: it is hard to establish an ongoing thread of communication from interview to interview when the client forgets after five minutes:

> Mr H (age 92) answered the door clad in pyjamas and dressing gown. He failed to remember me despite the fact that we have talked on a number of occasions and he apologised for this saying his memory is getting very bad and seems to be getting worse.

With this additional problem the danger of misunderstanding and misinterpretation is even greater.

What, then, are the possibilities, and some of the opportunities for reducing frustration and increasing communication with the blind, deaf or speechless older person?

The client's pace   The value of long-term and short-term work with older people will be discussed later. There are certainly special considerations in working with older people with sensory deprivation in terms of the speed with which relationships can be built up. It may be necessary to demonstrate continuing concern for the client by visiting and spending time with him, attempting to reach out on a very basic level—perhaps talking about very general topics— in order to build up channels of understanding. It may be possible to find practical ways of building these up:

> This week I took a box of dominoes with me. He immediately asked me for a cigarette and when I indicated that I hadn't any he lapsed into his usual moody silence. After a while I suggested we should play dominoes as he had once mentioned he used to play. After another long silence he agreed and after replying to my general questions in monosyllables he began to talk about his sisters.

Silence   One of the dangers of allowing the client to move at his own pace is that he may never quite understand the reason for the social worker's attentions. A further danger, and one that is also inherent in sharing silences with clients, is that going at too slow a pace may become frustrating or boring for the client and cause him to reject the relationship.

Many things happen during silences, and silences are common in work with the elderly because of the general slowing down of their speech and also because of sensory loss. Silences may be thoughtful, or they may be full of anger and rejection, or they may be full of care and concern. It is important to try to be aware of the messages contained in silence: messages that really rest on what has gone before and on the non-verbal factors in the silence: eye-contact, facial movements, body reactions, etc. If the client receives constant confirmation that his non-verbal messages are being understood he will feel more free to experiment and struggle with verbal methods. It is frustrating for both client and worker if words cannot be heard or formed but if the worker can show he has the patience to struggle and sufficient concern to wish to spend time in struggling the client may be encouraged to make a greater effort of concentration.

Sometimes, of course, patients use deafness and silence for defensive reasons: Mrs J was admitted to a long-stay geriatric ward from a private nursing home after her money had run out. The social worker reported during the first interview:

> Sister told me that Mrs J had become quite distressed on leaving the Nursing Home ... Mrs J in bed, quite deaf and very difficult to communicate with. This difficulty of communication was increased by the very withdrawn attitude of Mr J who was most unwilling to discuss anything concerning her affairs. She has apparently been subject to considerable stress in the last few months and has reacted by 'blocking-off' and now exists in a limbo of her own creation.

Fortunately in this case the social worker persisted and two months later was able to report:

> Saw Mrs J on the ward. I was able to communicate with her quite easily and the only difficulty was an indication of slight deafness on her part. She was mildly confused but this was probably due to her recent change of wards.

Touch The social and sexual implications of touch have complicated the social worker's attitude to touch as a communication method. Used appropriately and with full understanding touch may be a useful way of giving a message to the client: sometimes it is the only way:

Mrs K was of uncertain age: probably about 80. She lived alone in a detached house hidden behind a large hedge and in a wild garden. She had withdrawn from the community and only went to the post office and to the shops once a week. Her one surviving son lived ten miles away but rarely visited because she always became agitated and muddled when he came, and she made excited, paranoid accusations against him and his wife.

The social worker became involved after Mrs K visited the Housing Department and was unable to tell them why she had come. A letter arranging an appointment was sent but she denied receiving it and only after the third visit did she allow the social worker, a woman, into the house. She was very deaf, and this seemed complicated by a degree of dementia: she had paranoid feelings about her neighbours, with one exception, as well as about her son.

Varying from week to week she was confused in that she was unable to find words and names, was unaware of time and the past, and she sometimes threatened suicide. During the seventh visit to the house the social worker reported:

'I arrived at the house and could see Mrs K in the front room, wearing only her underclothes: I eventually made her hear and she let me in. . . . We talked about her son and she repeated her usual paranoid ideas about his wife and then became excited. . . . I had lost the thread of her conversation as she was stumbling over the words and hesitated often, missing out words. She could obviously see I couldn't understand and became very angry: she looked round in great agitation and suddenly burst into tears of frustration. I couldn't think of anything else to do so I put my arm round her shoulders. She held my hand for a while then stood up, dried her eyes and smiled weakly. She fetched a box from the cupboard and showed me it contained a lot of coins and pound notes: she said with great feeling: "Money." '

This situation may be open to many interpretations but there is no doubt that the social worker felt that the only way to contain this old lady's grief, anger and frustration was by physically holding her. After this interview Mrs K began to improve and was able to reach out herself after a while to take the worker's hand before she left the house at the end of visits—a mark, perhaps, not so much of gratitude but of trust:

'Overall, Mrs K has improved from not caring for herself and being muddled and suspicious and paranoid to being more alive in her personality; she is much less muddled and more inclined to trust people. Next week she has agreed to let me take her to see the doctor about a hearing aid.'

Practical aids to communication   Spectacles, hearing aids and false teeth are essential aids to enjoyment of life in old age and should not be neglected. It should be borne in mind that hearing aids have a lot of very real disadvantages: they are, for example, unable to select and differentiate between sounds. The result may be that in a busy hospital ward, or in a house full of noisy children, the old person finds the hearing aid a disadvantage in conducting a conversation. It is not necessarily true, therefore, that artificial aids are always beneficial but on the whole they are valuable additions to self respect. An old man whose teeth no longer fit properly may be reluctant to talk simply because his teeth do not fit properly and cause embarrassment. These practical factors should not be neglected.

Similarly it is important for the worker to introduce himself to the partially-sighted or blind clearly and distinctly. Unless this is done the client may not be aware of whom he is talking to and may be too embarrassed to ask.

Telephones may have a lot of advantages to offer to older people, especially those who live alone or are physically at risk. A project in Hull (Gregory and Young, 1972) found that the installation of telephones made a significant difference to the lives of older people. In particular an easing of all-round communication follows the provision of a telephone and for the housebound elderly this is an important contribution to making life more bearable.

Environment and communication   The actual physical environment in which an old person finds himself will predispose to good or bad communication. In his own home he may feel more at ease, more in control of the situation; alternatively he may be painfully aware of the poor condition of his home, the inadequacy of the heating, or the state of the garden and this could cause him to be hesitant and apologetic, or aggressive and hostile.

In a hospital ward, or other institutional environment, a client can feel at a disadvantage for many reasons: perhaps because he cannot rise to greet a visitor, or perhaps because he is badly dressed, or in night-clothes. The social worker's attitude and approach can do a lot to put the old person at his ease and help him talk.

Language and communication In a general sense, communication depends on the existence of language: this consists of words, signs and symbols. Some older people have never been able to acquire a very wide range of linguistic ability, either because of low intellectual ability, or through lack of social opportunity. Others tend to become less competent because of age-related changes (loss of attention, interest, etc.) or because of illness or disability.

Aphasia, associated with cerebrovascular accident, may present problems in so far as old people suffering from aphasia may be unable to find the words to use, or understand the words that others use in talking to them: they cannot send or receive messages. Some indications for treatment and approach are evident from a study conducted at the University of Kiowa (Stoicheff, 1960). Three groups of aphasic patients were subject to varying stimulation: positive encouragement, active discouragement (a friendly but disappointed attitude being adopted), and a neutral approach in which they were neither encouraged nor discouraged. Although the three groups started on an equal footing, at the end of only three days those in the 'encouraged' group performed significantly better than those in the 'discouraged' group, with the 'neutral' group somewhere in between but closer to those in the 'encouraged' group.

The inference would seem to be that friendly encouragement and persistence with clients who have physically-based language difficulties will contribute to their long-term communication ability.

General commentary Communication is a process of gathering information and attaching meanings to it. It will be affected by subjective needs in the social worker and is especially complex in working with some elderly clients who experience visual, linguistic or hearing loss. In overcoming these difficulties the social worker may have to be more flexible in his approach to communication with elderly clients than with younger clients. Silence, touch and above all patience and determination are needed to stay with the older person while he struggles to make himself understood. If this struggle is shared the client will feel encouraged to continue his attempts to communicate. Equally important is the need to be aware of practical aids to communication—hearing and visual aids especially—and to understand the problems and difficulties of using them. Communication is an essential part both of building and maintaining a relationship: without it emotions and anxieties cannot be clarified and the true nature of conflict cannot be understood.

CONFLICT

One common approach to social work with older people has been on the basis of a conflict model. Crisis in work with the elderly is often seen in rather confused terms, as a combination of emergency need for practical services and a conflict in community attitudes. Before the real nature of the work can be examined it will be necessary to look at the concepts of conflict, consensus, crisis and emergency.

Conflict, consensus and power   The sociological approach has taken two main forms. Weber (1947) saw power as the ability of one person to carry out his will in the face of opposition and resistance from other people. This approach tends to see hostility as inherent in the power relationship and ignores the fact that power relationships can be relationships of mutual convenience (the baby, again, has power, and experiences the power of others but aggression is not an essential component of the relationship); it tends also to see power as a property that belongs in the individual whereas it exists only as a capacity in the individual and as a property of the relationship (Martin, 1971).

Blau (1967) has extended this approach in a discussion of the nature of exchanges and pleasure in social life. He suggests that the roots of most human pleasures and of most suffering are to be found in the exchange of social rewards (although he excludes the irrational push of emotional forces which are not goal-orientated). Social exchange, in Blau's terms, may reflect any behaviour orientated to socially mediated goals. On the one hand he describes reciprocal (two-sided) relationships which, when intrinsically satisfying (i.e. meeting inner needs) lead to mutual attraction, and when extrinsically satisfying (i.e. receiving social rewards) lead to exchange. On the other hand unilateral relationships receiving intrinsic rewards lead to one-sided attachment and when receiving extrinsic rewards lead to power.

In this approach conflict may be a property of a relationship in which power to obtain social rewards is one-sided. Parsons (1967), on the other hand, tries to avoid the conflict approach and views power as a system resource—in terms of obligations, mutuality and negative sanctions. In other words he puts consensus in the place of conflict—but ignores the fact that power is always held over somebody.

On a more individual level theories of personality development have commonly described opposing forces. Freud (1937) suggested that instincts are divided into two groups, the erotic which try to collect together living substances to create larger unities, and the death instincts which act against that tendency. On the surface this appears to propose a situation of unending conflict but the development of personality is dependent on the synthesis of these opposing positions. Growth comes out of the synthesis of opposites within the personality. In circumstances where synthesis is incomplete conflict arises.

The inference seems to be that on all levels of interaction, both on individual as well as the wider social levels, conflict may exist. In relationships conflict may be the result of inequitable power balances. Within the individual, conflict may result from a variety of causes, including the failure to balance inner forces and the failure to match inner needs to external circumstances.

Social work and the elderly—conflict or consensus? It has been suggested (Knott, 1972) that a conflict orientation would serve to clarify some of the functional aspects of conflict as they relate to the dyadic casework relationship. Social work and the elderly has been largely tied up in thinking about the dysfunctional aspects of working with older people. It may be (Bumagin, 1972) that old people are seen as 'difficult', or 'depressed'; 'old people's frailties are irreversible', 'old people are boring', 'help for old people is limited by inadequate resources', etc. The implications of these viewpoints are primarily negative and conflict is seen as existing within the old person (depression, hostility), between social worker and elderly client (old people are boring, difficult), and between the elderly client, the social worker and the resource base.

Hostility often exists in very exaggerated form in situations including the elderly. Usually this is because of lack of resources on the one hand and the fact that families care for the elderly relatives until they reach breaking point (in most cases) on the other. This hostility associated with conflict is not necessarily dysfunctional and may have a positive contribution to make to growth and change—although conflict may also result in destruction and damage. The task of social workers in working with the elderly is to become involved in situations of conflict, to reduce the dysfunctional aspects of the conflict and encourage and clarify the functional aspect. Two important functions of conflict are evident: (i) conflict contributes to the maintenance of relationships between the individual and his environment, between social groups and between societies: it helps to establish and maintain identity; (ii) conflict stimulates behaviour change and the establishment of new roles, norms, and institutions in social situations.

It is important also to remember in forming an assessment of the individual and the social situation that there is a difference between conflict as a means to an end and conflict as an end in itself. To identify the reasons for the existence of conflict is essential: conflict is not necessarily bad in so far as it contributes to healthy change or in so far as it helps to maintain an equilibrium through which the individual can continue to progress along the ageing continuum. A concept of equilibrium—or balance of power—does not inevitably have to be a static concept.

In the practical situation assessment of the conflict will depend on the establishment of good communication and understanding, and will lead to a decision on the nature of the action to be taken. The action will be relevant to the elderly client in so far as it contributes to his ability to proceed with a normal, satisfying process of ageing.

Crisis and emergency   In social work terms a crisis is a block to the achievement of important life-goals with which the client is unable to cope without help. A crisis may therefore be long-standing and of gradual onset, such as in the case of an arthritic old lady who has become unable to do her own shopping over a few years, or the family who have provided long-term nursing care, without help or relief, for an elderly parent and find they can no longer cope. Alternatively a crisis can be of sudden onset, such as the need for care following a stroke, or other crisis illness, or the death of a close relative, etc. A large part of the confusion of seeing social work with the elderly as conflict-orientated has stemmed from the fact that 'crisis' often becomes mixed up with 'emergency' and is seen, under pressure, as dysfunctional.

An emergency is a problem that demands an immediate solution: a crisis may involve emergency action but is fundamentally concerned with the past, present and the future, not just the current emergency. Very often presenting problems are made up not of the older person's view but of the perceptions of those around him. The so-called 'crisis' takes on a life of its own and begins to move away from the actual client and becomes a muddle of other people's projections and misperceptions (Brearley, 1972).

The solution to this difficulty is good communication, and full assessment which will distinguish between the healthy and the unhealthy situation. A total assessment, with an understanding of the functional and dysfunctional nature of conflict situations, is the only basis for treatment planning in social work and older people. If communication is inadequate, and assessment is incomplete, the treatment response will be to the presenting problem which may not be the real need. The lack of resources and the pressure of demand may push social workers into inappropriate emergency action on a superficial level and irreversible action is often taken : admission to institutional care and selling of the home and furniture being the extreme example.

5

Relationships

Whether it be the closely controlled relationship between the social worker and client in the narrowly defined one-to-one casework situation, or the relationship he builds up with family groups, treatment groups, or community groups, the basic essential for the social worker is the relationship. It is this, in particular, that distinguishes him from other caring professionals. In using the interaction between worker and client consciously and in a controlled way for social treatment purposes the social worker is able to help the client with the problems that most concern him in the social situation in which he finds himself.

In building up a relationship with the older person several points are especially important. It is, for example, essential to recognise the difficulties of communication that have already been described. In addition, the elderly experience loss and a shrinking life-space as well as a decrease in the amount of energy available to invest in relationships. In building a relationship the social worker will have to be prepared to move at the client's own pace, within the limitations of his energies, concentration, attention, interest and ability to absorb new experiences. There is, too, always the possibility that the social worker may slip into the role of a substitute son or daughter or grandchild (Goldberg, Mortimer and Williams, 1970). Emphasis tends to be on the reduction of environmental pressures which prevent the achievement of satisfying ageing and rather less on the modification of attitudes and feelings about environmental pressures, although the latter must definitely not be ignored.

One further general consideration in work with the elderly is the attitude of the worker himself to old age, physical disability and death. Social workers often tend to have a negative attitude to old age (Blank, 1971), in common with laymen and other professionals involved in work with the elderly, and even old people themselves.

The role of old person is not a popular one and the physically or mentally deteriorated old person may present social workers with the necessity of thinking about old age in personal terms. If a worker is unable to handle his own feelings about death, deterioration, and loss then to discuss the client's feelings about them may cause anxiety for the worker. There is a real danger of colluding in a denial of the existence of some problems. It has already been suggested that most older people have faced and resolved their own fears of death and many social work clients do have an apparently realistic (though possibly depressive) attitude—'I'm very tired. I wish God would come for me'; 'I wish I could go now and be with my husband'; etc. Nevertheless grief and mourning are a major part of adjustment to ageing and the social worker must be able to handle these without undue anxiety.

Some of these general points need to be extended and clarified and linked with the previous discussions of the ageing process, assessment and communication.

SOCIAL WORK AND THE INDIVIDUAL

Ego-adaptation

The ego has several major functions, growing out of the conflict-synthesis task that it performs within the individual. It mediates between the id and reality, and between the id and the superego, and generally plays a synthesising role. In addition to this the ego plays an executive role in relation to perception, intention, thinking, language, etc., and ego-adaptation rests in the mastery of the reality of the self-in-the-situation.

Being an old person implies having had the strength and ability to live through a long life and therefore implies an ability to change and adapt to changing external surroundings. In old age the adaptive task of the ego involves adjustment, typically, to: (1) the loss of social roles and status (retirement, etc.); (2) the loss of physical capacities and the knowledge of death; (3) the loss of significant relationships: in one sense the removal of significant object relations and consequently (4) the loss of channels of expression and emotional satisfaction with fewer opportunities to substitute new channels.

Reaction to these losses may take a number of maladaptive forms, some of which have already been examined. Regression to earlier levels of behaviour which provided more satisfactions is one way in which the ego defends against change. Denial of the reality of the situation is also a possibility, as is the projection of fears and anxieties on to others, or on to the outside world. The sublimation of energies is less commonly seen, perhaps because energy is less available, but over-reaction to situations and the taking up of rigid, entrenched positions on, for instance, racial issues is not uncommon.

In helping the older person to overcome his neurotic defences the social worker is, by definition, helping him to change and grow. In this sense casework goals with the elderly client can sometimes be realistically aiming at ego-modification. However, this will be much more rare than in work with younger people partly because most problems are concerned with finding substitutes for environmental losses but partly because of the time factor. Some techniques of ego-modifying help require more time than the old person has available—elderly clients are more likely to die.

Transference in relationships Every relationship contains two elements in varying degrees. One aspect of the relationship rests on the ability of one person to perceive the reality of another: to see his objective qualities, faults, abilities and to react to them appropriately in the current situation. Another aspect of relationships is that of transference: the tendency to see one person in a situation in an inappropriate way—to project the image of any person who has been important in the past, on to another. This tendency to transform the present person and the present situation into the image of an earlier person in a previously experienced situation leads to problems of perception, distortion, inappropriate reactions, and manipulative actions.

In the transference situation two particular alternative attitudes are reproduced (Storr, 1960). The person who sees himself as being vulnerable will react either by becoming clinging and dependent on those who appear to be able to protect and contain him, or by rejecting those who are in a caring role, seeing them as threatening to engulf him. The fear of abandonment leads to clinging, and the fear of loss of independent existence leads to rejection and aloofness.

Primarily, in a transference situation the therapist is given the role of parent and behaviour is linked to this. Age and sex do not appear to play a major part in this and there seems to be no reason why a young male social worker should not be seen in a mothering role by an elderly lady. Older people have usually learned to experience parenting, or aspects of parenting, from other relationships—husband, wife, son or daughter—and it is not unlikely that the social worker being placed in the role of son, daughter, or grandchild will receive demands for both the real content of the role (weekly visits, shopping, support, etc.), as well as parenting demands:

Mr and Mrs L were in their middle 80s when Mr L had a slight stroke and began to attend at a day hospital. They had been married for sixty-five years and were very close, both being determined to stay together as long as possible. The male social worker visited them, usually at home, every week for three months until Mr L was admitted to hospital as his wife could no longer care for him. During this time the worker helped them in a number of practical ways. He was also able to give them emotional support through regular discussions which helped them clarify their thoughts and feelings and recognise his concern for them.

Soon after Mr L was admitted to hospital their son died and Mr L deteriorated rapidly and died. During his early visits to Mrs L after her husband's death help was on a practical level:

'Mrs L seems to manage all the chores without any difficulty, although I was able to reassemble the electric fire for her. . . . She has now received the Supplementary Benefit and I have also made arrangements for her Widow's Benefit.'

At this time the worker was filling the role of son, and to some extent of husband. When he had to leave the area a few weeks later other elements that had developed began to crystallise:

'Mrs L seen at home. She was quite distressed at learning I would be leaving next week and will require continuing contact. She undoubtedly feels a strong sense of loss at this new turn of events and needs to re-adjust to the idea of creating new relationships whilst containing the elements of "transference" which she has associated with my presence and former male figures in her life.'

Two further points emerge here. At a time of emotional stress or crisis people are more vulnerable—a truism, but nevertheless important. The second point is that transference may be matched by counter-transference: social workers do enjoy working with some clients more than others and become attached to them, viewing some aspects of the situation subjectively. So in this situation the worker felt guilty at leaving his dependent client and insisted she needed continuing social work help. As one social worker put it: 'When I changed jobs, there was one old lady I nearly brought with me.'

There may, in fact, be a case for the acceptance of a parental role in working with some elderly patients. To attempt to work with the transference and to interpret it to the elderly client would be to provoke insights that may not be necessary or helpful. Mrs L would not have benefited from being told that she saw the social worker as a father, or husband, or son: what she needed was a reliable, dependable figure to cling to while she grew to be able to cope alone again. To accept the transference—as long as it is fully understood and used in a controlled way—will be to allow elderly clients to act out their needs in a safe, dependable way. If they can do this they can often feel able to take a new look at the world from a relatively safe base and begin to move towards it in a new way.

Past, present and future It has been suggested earlier that the achievement of 'ego-integrity' involves the individual in being able to see the past as good and inevitable and therefore the present as unchangeable and acceptable. If this can be achieved then death is also accepted as unchanging, inevitable and therefore not to be feared.

To help the elderly client to achieve this view of his past life will be to help him achieve the final stage of maturity, and, hopefully, satisfaction within himself. There are some very real barriers to this in our society as a whole. Concepts of alienation and anomia (Tunstall, 1966) suggest that many people in an industrialised society feel no link with production—to look back on a lifetime of punching out washers on a production line for someone else can hardly hold the same satisfaction that exists for a craftsman who owns his own business and sells his own product. A further problem is the difficulty of seeing the links between the goals that are acceptable to society and the socially available ways of achieving those goals.

Several ways are open to the social worker to help an elderly client to begin to see the order and sequence of his past life and to relate it to his current situation. Caring support and concern, combined with the opportunity to talk about the past and clarify past and present patterns, are important. Reminiscence, too, is an important asset in therapy. Religious guidance might appropriately be brought in for some older people to help them understand (and feel) the order of things.

Discussion of death may also help: old people may have very often accepted the fact of death but may welcome the opportunity to ask for information about the pain that may go with death and about practical services that are available to offset problems of dying. They may wish to express feelings about death and also review arrangements for their burial, and the disposal of their homes and personal belongings. If these facts and feelings can be clarified they can often clear the way for the elderly client to begin to turn his mind and energies to thinking about other problem areas.

It would be wrong to assume, then, that old people cannot achieve a good deal of ego-adaptation. However, it is only very rarely that they require the prompting of 'insight' : usually adaptation is to loss and external pressure. Transference does exist in all relationships but rarely needs to be interpreted to the elderly client : providing a dependable parent-figure can often help him act out his needs and release energy for suitable adaptation. Most important of all is the recognition that each relationship is between two individuals and each will have his own particular needs : flexibility is of fundamental importance.

Overcoming current environmental pressures

Working with the individual within his current environmental situation is at the heart of all social work. Material deprivation, physical loss, poverty and loss of social supports characterise the situation of the older person. Social workers are most commonly involved in helping to overcome these problems, particularly in terms of the lack of resources that are available to compensate.

Short-term, or long-term involvement? Traditionally casework has been seen as a long-term therapy in which a relationship is developed and support is given to the client over a long period. Recent studies (Reid and Shyne, 1969; Reid and Epstein, 1972) have challenged this in so far as they have shown that families receiving only a limited period of help made more progress than those receiving long-term help. Other studies (Mayer and Timms, 1970; Timms, 1973) have tended to confirm that clients are more likely to respond positively to active, goal-directed social work than they do to passive, explanatory, clarifying techniques. One important study did show a relationship between intervention of trained (as opposed to untrained) caseworkers with elderly clients and the likelihood of extended social interaction, improved morale, and improved attitudes to their social situation (Goldberg, Mortimer and Williams, 1970).

On the whole old people, or those who refer their needs, will request practical services that they can see and describe. This may be phrased as, 'I am old and so I need to go into an old people's home', or it may be put more vaguely as, 'I need help because I am disabled'. However it is expressed the referral usually implies a ready-made diagnosis and the expectation of a limited range of treatments. Often a full assessment of the situation will reveal that the problem is not specific but has arisen as a result of a gradual accumulation of minor irritants that reach such a pitch that the old person can no longer function appropriately. An intensive short-term input of social work will consist of assessment, with some attempt to affect attitudes to the situation, but more especially an injection of practical help and resources. In this way the old person can be helped back to an acceptable functioning level (back to the normal process of ageing) in a relatively short time.

The requirement is essentially for skilled assessment, short-term casework involvement, practical help and then, after reasonable functioning is restored, the situation will no longer require the skilled social worker. It will certainly, however, require some form of continuing involvement—perhaps a voluntary visitor, or perhaps a home help. Who ever does take on this role must be educated to recognise difficulties almost before they begin and to report back to the social worker if things do start to go wrong.

Mrs M was 70 and suffered from a multitude of disabilities of which osteo-arthritis was the primary one. She was referred by her GP to a day hospital and was seen by the social worker:

'She is a very talkative old lady with a good memory and a wish to discuss her problems freely : her impairments are the main focus of her interest. She told me her husband died six years ago and since then she has lived in several rented flats before moving to her present warden-controlled one. . . .

She says she can no longer get to the shops or into town and feels lonely and isolated and wants to get into an old people's home.'

A few days later the worker visited the flat:

'Client's flat spotlessly clean and well furnished, she is obsessively tidy and is well served by a home help who cheerfully meets all her needs. . . . Later I saw the warden who described Mrs M as a cantankerous, difficult old woman who had every opportunity to join in community social activities but would not do so. He also mentioned that her son often calls on her as he works in the area.'

Objectively Mrs M had little cause to complain. Her disabilities were found to be less serious than she insisted, her family gave her a lot of help, a home help did a lot of her work and the neighbours were readily available. Never-

theless, since the death of her husband she had become
in-turned and complaining and was unable to break out of
her rut. Attendance at the day hospital for a month
included four long interviews with the social worker during
which he was able to help her by reflecting back some of
her own feelings and attitudes for her inspection and
clarification. Practical help was also given in the form of
assistance with financial problems, and arrangements for
adaptations to the flat. After five weeks of intensive
team input at the day hospital the social worker was able
to report:

'When I called she was having her hair done by a hairdresser
who visits the flats. She gazed blankly at me and then
asked why I'd come. She obviously felt I was no longer
any use to her and after telling me about her trip into town
on the bus the previous day she said she didn't think
she'd bother to go to the hospital this week.'

Not all cases are as nicely rounded as this one, of course, but it
does serve to illustrate the way in which short-term, intensive intervention can help people out of the vicious circle of withdrawal and
rejection in which they sometimes find themselves.

Caring support and concern One important aspect of working
with the elderly is their need to be 'held'. Sometimes this will
involve touch; often it means a less physical, emotional reaching-
out to them. Most people need to be valued and to receive affection
but sometimes older people have outlived those who met this need
for them. To receive personal warmth and feel valued is a basic
need: sometimes the social worker may have to give these to his
elderly client, fulfilling what is essentially a social role. This is not
to suggest that all he should do is care for the older person: if
love and affection is all that is required many non-social work
resources are available. Nevertheless the needs of isolated, elderly
clients may be tied up with their lack of 'tender loving care' and
part of the development of a helping relationship will be the
provision of this care and concern.

Before a person can feel fully understood he has to feel that he
is valued and before he can feel valued and accept affection and
concern he must feel that he has been understood. Caring for the
elderly client is inextricably linked with the process of learning
about him.

Discussion of present difficulties One reason for talking to clients is to assess their needs. Equally important, along with the social worker's need to understand the client's current situation, is the client's own need to understand. Discussion of present difficulties in the environmental situation will help a client to begin to perceive the reality of his environment and of the pressures on him. In the isolation that ageing may sometimes bring the reality of the outside world may loom larger than life: paranoid ideas about neighbours or families often present themselves. To bring the ideas into the open, and to talk with another person, will often be to clarify them.

Through the discussion of the current life-situation the old person can begin to look for the patterns and processes of his life. Liton and Olstein (1969) have discussed the important part that reminiscence can play in identifying the meaning of the past and the pattern in the older person's whole life-span. They suggest that reminiscence, by acting as a way of encouraging attention from others, can make an elderly client feel valued and more of a person. Beyond this they also suggest that reminiscence is an important tool in therapy as the client is encouraged to relive his memory and reach further into his past.

Undoubtedly older people tend to look to the past and review past satisfactions and listening to reminiscences is a useful way of building up a picture of the elderly person. The things he has done in the past, the kind of person he has been, the way he feels about his life and his experiences become clearer through a free-flowing reminiscence. Most people escape into day-dreaming from time to time—what would we do if we won a lot of money, what would we say if we were offered promotion, etc.? Current life-pressures and dissatisfactions may be handled more easily if day-dreaming is possible. Old people are no exception and if they are encouraged to look for past satisfactions this may help them cope with every-day dissatisfactions. It will also help them learn about themselves and their purpose in life—to help them towards ego-integrity, or adaptation to the idea of old age and death.

Liton and Olstein have gone as far as saying that a relationship between social worker and elderly client that uses reminiscence to its full extent will be comparable to that between patient and therapist in the analytical situation. The justification for this seems rather dubious but it does again raise the point that early life is an essential component of work with older clients. Using reminiscence to identify the past, to demonstrate interest in the client, and to encourage the reliving of previous satisfactions, will all contribute to a better understanding of the present. It is also worth commenting that looking back on a satisfying life may give strength but looking back on disappointments in the past may have the opposite effect. It will be necessary to control the nature and extent of reminiscence to minimise this aspect.

Presentation of resources The present situation will always be partly dependent on the past because attitudes are rooted in previously learned behaviour. It is important to understand this link in helping the elderly client to adjust to loss, dependence, etc., and also in helping him to accept practical help in the form of material resources.

Accepting help is often not an easy process and older people may see money, or practical help, as 'charity'; partly, this is based on earlier attitudes to charitable gifts. One possible result is the need of elderly clients to give presents to social workers. This is usually for many interrelated reasons but may be partly a wish to restore the balance of power in the relationship, and partly a confusion over the social worker's role. In giving practical help the social worker must be flexible in his approach to the elderly client and in his use of the resources at his disposal. Some fundamental criteria for the use of practical resources can be identified (Milloy, 1964).

(1) How far will the use of the resource increase or help to maintain the client's capacity for mastery?

(2) How far will the use of the resource tend to reduce his sense of isolation and increase his feeling of being needed?

(3) How far will the resource contribute to the client's protection?

Grief, loss and bereavement

Loss is central to social work with the elderly and an understanding of the implications of loss at a wide range of levels will be necessary. Loss may come suddenly and without warning, as in the loss of a friend, or relative. It may come as the result of an accumulation of minor, gradual losses but sometimes creep up almost unnoticed.

Helping the old person to adjust to his losses is therefore the underlying approach of social work with the elderly. A crisis that is presented almost always contains some elements of loss. Returning to Mrs L, after the death of her husband a number of typical aspects of work with grieving clients were reported by the social worker:

'She intends to stay on in her own home for as long as possible and she likes the familiar environment which she shared with her husband for so long. This provides her with a valuable defence against a feeling of total loss which she might otherwise have experienced and helps her preserve her own independence.... Needs help with finances and I have asked DHSS to assess for Supplementary Benefit and have also applied for rate rebate on her behalf.'

The need to remain in a safe, familiar environment while the confusion begins to sort itself out, as well as the need for practical help in organisation, are often evident. On the subsequent visit:

'Mrs L rather depressed, having begun to experience a true sense of loss following her husband's death. She has entered a critical period of re-adjustment but fortunately has frequent contact with her daughters. She has a great need to discuss her own feelings and requires a sensitive appreciation of her problems to help work through the great change in her life, after so many years of marriage.'

A successful process of grieving requires that someone should be available to 'hold' the grieving person; to be depended on while feelings are discussed and relieved through sharing. It is vital that relatives are not frightened away by grief and they may require support themselves and encouragement to visit the bereaved person to continue this holding.

Protection

In a few cases the social worker may be involved in making a decision about a client's ability to reach an appropriate decision about his own safety. Sometimes mental confusion prevents the elderly person from being able to look after himself and it may even be that he is a danger to himself—leaving gas on, drying clothes on an electric fire, leaving kettles boiling for hours, etc. In this context the moral and ethical considerations seem less relevant than the need, again, for a flexible and sensitive application of compulsion. The compulsory removal of an old person to care carries real physical dangers to health and if emotional equilibrium can be preserved through a supportive relationship the dangers will be lessened.

SOCIAL WORK AND THE FAMILY

Some aspects of the special problems of families with an ageing member have already been considered. Two of the particular aspects

75

that are often presented to social workers are conflict and scape-goating.

Conflict often results from the real, intolerable burdens that many families cope with to extreme lengths. It may also result from long-standing internal family interactions which flare up because of increased loss, dependence, or merely enforced closeness. If old people are rejected by their families this may sometimes be because they have never been able to care for their families and are seen as undeserving of love. More often it is force of circum-stances that creates rejection—the burden cannot be shouldered any longer without help.

In working with the family group the social worker is usually free to use techniques of family group therapy that are appropriate to all family situations. One aspect of work with the family group rather than with one individual is that communication links are greatly increased in number and complexity. If the old person does suffer from a degree of sensory loss then his participation in group interviews is inhibited.

'When I first arrived I was shown in to the front room which seemed damp and was obviously not used often. Mr N was not present....
I felt at this time that Mr N should be present but when I suggested he should be involved they resisted and said that even if I shouted he wouldn't understand me. I pressed them and eventually we all went into the living room. When we finally sat down I realised that Mr N's chair was so arranged that he was effectively excluded from direct eye contact with anyone else in the room.'

Controlling, directing, and interpreting in this situation makes even greater demands on the social worker.

Working with marital difficulties between elderly couples usually means working with relationships in which long-term, entrenched positions have been taken up. Sometimes the relationship is upset by an imbalance in the rate of ageing. If one partner, for example, suffers a disabling illness, or if one is unable to accept limited capacities, or the children have left the home, stress may occur:

At the age of 53 Mr O had a cardiovascular accident with a right hemiplegia but recovered sufficiently to return to work as an electrician. Seven years later he began to feel ill again and was eventually admitted to hospital. After several weeks the ward sister referred him to the social worker with a request for an assessment of the home

circumstances and discharge plans. Although Mrs O showed
some hostility at the suggestion that he should return
home, ostensibly because she was in part-time employment
and Mr O was not mobile, it was felt that this immobility
was the result of apathy (by implication: laziness?) and
that he should return home with day hospital attendance.
After a further two months this plan was carried out.
The day hospital social worker visited his wife and 'she was
at first rather aggressive in manner but having unburdened
herself became tearful and apologetic for her outburst'.
It emerged during this first interview that Mrs O had recently
had a hysterectomy and had been unable to grieve for
this loss before being faced with the loss of at least a part of
her husband. She felt that during all her previous contacts
with the hospital she had been seen as a bad woman who
did not care enough for her husband because she had
expressed doubts about taking him home. This feeling of being
blamed was partly a projection of her own guilt at feeling
angry and rejecting towards him. There is also no doubt
that hospital staff had colluded in seeing her as an uncaring
person.

The social worker found herself with several immediate tasks:
firstly Mrs O was asking for (albeit non-verbally) a recognition of
her own needs in the situation and she needed the opportunity to
grieve for her various losses. An acceptance of her anger towards
Mr O and displaced anger directed at hospital workers eventually
helped her to perceive the reality of her situation. In allowing her
to cry, and to mourn for lost parts of herself, the worker helped
her to cope with these losses. She was aided in this by the fact
that the O's son emigrated during the development of the relationship and helping them both to grieve for their son helped them
reassess and mourn for their earlier losses. Mr O himself also needed
help in adjusting to his loss and his changed physical self. A difficulty in speech and emotional lability complicated communication, but by fixing on the practical issue of his son's emigration,
and bringing books about the country he had gone to, she was
able to build up a trusting relationship. Through the relationship
she demonstrated her care for his difficulties as well as giving him
both the opportunity to think clearly about the changes in his life
and to reassess them, and the impetus to look outside himself at
new interests and activities.
Over a five-month period the worker was able to present a constant front to repeated expressions of ambivalence from Mrs O.

Sometimes this took the form of aggression towards 'the welfare', sometimes resentment of the way Mr O responded to the worker and did things he wouldn't do when she wasn't there (walking with an aid, etc.), and sometimes an excessive welcome, or giving presents. By remaining constant in the face of these variations the worker gradually showed she accepted the whole of Mrs O and was able to build a useful relationship through which she helped Mrs O not only at home but with a crisis situation in her job.

A further aspect of the social work task involved helping other workers to understand the needs of Mrs O. One of the difficulties of the caring situation is the possibility of rivalry over patients or clients—the 'Whose child is this?' situation. In helping to clarify the dynamics of the problem the worker could present Mrs O as an individual rather than a scapegoat and help to take some of the pressure from her.

By the end of the period the social worker had been able to work with Mr and Mrs O in terms of their individual emotional needs and also in terms of the change in the focus of the marital relationship. She had been able to help with their practical situation through arranging day centre attendance, home help, attendance allowance, etc., and she had helped the caring team to see the totality of Mr O's life. This work, however, took place against a background of medical treatment and rehabilitation and teamwork was an essential component. If Mr O was able to walk and take an interest in life this was not just because of drugs, or physiotherapy, or a casework relationship but because of a team approach to his total needs.

In a family situation the elderly parent may be the cause or the symptom of conflict. The indications for whole group family treatment are in these situations where the needs of the old person cause stress throughout the generations of the family. Particularly important is the situation in which the middle generation parent has been unable to emancipate himself from his own parents. The parent with the unresolved problem of emancipation (usually the wife) is caught between her role of dependent child to her own parent, who is seen as omnipotent, and her role as adult wife and mother (Wasser, 1966). If the wife is unable to resolve her own relationship problem when her children are small the problem will often become more intense as the children grow to adolescence and seek emancipation themselves. Unresolved conflicts of this nature may be clarified and progress made in family group interviews.

In all family situations it is impossible to ignore, for diagnostic purposes, the older parent within the family. Therapeutic approaches to any individual member of the family will affect the entire group functioning and the whole family background to the elderly client's problems must be examined.

OLD PEOPLE IN GROUPS

There are some special facets that older people bring to groups. A general insecurity and anxiety, associated with fear of death and, more practically, with reduced abilities, is common among elderly clients. They will fear groups if they expect to be unable to see or hear what is going on, or if they know they will be physically unable to sit for long. This leads into another problem—the poor self-image of older clients. A more pressing difficulty is often the poor mobility, and lack of transport that means groups of elderly clients are often only available in institutional settings. Fortunately the increase of day care facilities is bringing more opportunities for work with older people in client groups.

The usefulness of such groups is broad, but relatively little work has been done in such situations, in comparison to the traditional casework approach. Some of the values might be: (i) supplying social roles; (ii) encouraging esteem and self-valuing: strength can be drawn from peers in the current situation as well as from past achievements, often shared or partly held in common; and (iii) encouraging self-direction and individuality through allowing action to be taken by the individual on his own behalf. Exploration, and sharing of practical ways of coping with life-pressures are also possible.

Less commonly the group process may be used in: (iv) supporting existing personality strengths; and (v) occasional remedial ego-building. One positive thing that can be said about the use of group situations with elderly clients is that there is considerable scope for experiment. The extension of the use of groups will, hopefully, bring valuable results (Field, 1972).

6

Using practical resources

Advice, guidance and the provision of practical, material aid are a major part of the social work task in so far as they relate to situations of social dysfunction. Providing a material service is the job of the social worker if it is of relevance to his clients' abilities to function autonomously and, as they feel, appropriately in social situations, and if it is relevant in helping the client to feel a part of the whole society.

The important consideration is that each individual client should have his needs met without threat to his own ability to control the direction of his life. This will imply, as has already been discussed, a full assessment of total need: self-direction requires emotional and physical health as well as social capacities and offering these to older clients usually involves the presentation of practical resources. Much has already been said about the flexible use of resources. What are the resources, and what is meant by 'flexible use'?

HISTORICAL PERSPECTIVE

Welfare services for the elderly have sprung up in widely differing societies and cultures in many forms. Almost a thousand years ago in Britain care for the frail elderly was beginning to be provided by some churches and monasteries in a very limited way. The growth of 'hospitals' for the elderly was supported by the Church until the reign of Henry VIII when much of the provision disappeared during the dissolution of the monasteries. The result was an increase in vagrancy and a growth in the number of beggars. The first time the government took any positive part in the relief of general poverty and distress was in dealing with the stated problem of 'vagabonds and beggars' in a statute of 1531. This gave power to local officials to seek out, register and provide for those in need, and in 1536 a further enactment defined the nature of provision.

By the end of the sixteenth century the foundation of the Poor Law had been established and its provisions were codified in the Poor Law Act of 1601. A tradition of local relief of poverty and economic distress was established: the overseer of the poor had a responsibility for administering the provision of relief in the form of work for the unemployed, apprenticeships for children and assistance for the poor—including the elderly. This provision also included accommodation, eventually developed as workhouses.

By the beginning of the industrial revolution agricultural wages were very low, largely because of enclosures of land and displacement of labour. After 1795 many parishes began to give outdoor relief related to the price of bread and the size of families to supplement wages which were below starvation. The confusion between wage-earning and pauperism that was contained in this practice led eventually to the Poor Law Amendment Act of 1834.

Under this Act grouping together of parishes into Unions made larger operating areas possible and administration was simplified. One important aspect of the new law was the lack of any concept of social obligation. What lay behind the Poor Law at this time was a wish to remove the abuses that had been inherent in the early system rather than to encourage a new prosperity or quality of life for the poorer classes—a negative approach.

It was not for another hundred years that the idea of payment to old people as of right began to crystallise. In 1908 the first non-contributory old age pension was established and in 1925 the principle of social insurance was introduced in the form of contributory pensions.

Nevertheless, voluntary provision for the elderly still provided a large part of the relief, particularly through trusts and residential homes.

The Welfare State—developments after 1945

After the Second World War, development of services provided by the state for the elderly took four main forms.

(a) The National Insurance Act of 1946 replaced contributory old age pensions by a retirement pension paid to all who retired from active employment; provision was also made for an increased pension to be paid to those who continued to work after retirement age. The Ministry of National Insurance was established to run the service.

(b) The National Health Service Acts set out to create community services for health, provided by the local authorities, which would attend to the needs of the whole household. Health visitors, home nursing services, domestic help, chiropody and laundry for people suffering from illness were all within the scope of these Acts.

(c) The National Assistance Act of 1948 gave the local authorities power to make payments to voluntary organisations to provide services for the disabled and elderly in their own homes. It also placed a duty on them to provide residential accommodation for 'persons who by reason of age, infirmity, or any other circumstances are in need of care and attention which is not otherwise available to them'. The power to promote the welfare of people who were 'blind, deaf or dumb, and other persons who are substantially and permanently handicapped'—of whom a large proportion are elderly—was also contained in this Act.

(d) Housing authorities can exercise power under the Housing Acts to provide suitable housing for the elderly. For a number of reasons, especially lack of capital and equipment, early development was slow but after the 1949 Housing Act, which removed restrictions on providing housing for other than lower income groups, sheltered housing provision began to increase.

The development of services was patchy throughout the country and was, in the early post-war years and well into the 1950s, hindered by the lack of money and the shortage of building materials and resources in general.

As these difficulties began to ease, a discussion of the appropriateness of 'community care' played a major part in the development of services for old age. The Phillips Committee (1954), for instance, recommended that as far as possible old people should be allowed to remain in the community. A growing impetus towards the concept of community care came from the 1959 Mental Health Act and the development of long-term planning of services. In 1962 the local authorities were asked to prepare ten-year development plans for their health and welfare services. A Ministry circular (2/62) advised that: 'Services for the elderly should be designed to help them to remain in their own homes for as long as possible. For this purpose adequate supporting services must be available, including home nurses, domestic help, chiropody and temporary residential care.' The same circular went on to suggest that 'residential homes are required for those who, for some reason, short of a need for hospital care, cannot manage on their own, even in special housing with a resident warden'.

The growth of domiciliary resources continued to run alongside an increase in residential provision, from converted property in the early post-war years through purpose built, fairly large homes

(60 beds) and the smaller homes (30 beds). In 1962 Townsend's attack (Townsend, 1962) on the extensive use of residential resources encouraged an increase in domiciliary services.

More recently the Health Services and Public Health Act, under Section 45, made a general provision for the promotion of the welfare of the elderly and also imposed, under Section 13, a duty for local authorities to provide an adequate home help service, specifically including the handicapped in provision. The Chronically Sick and Disabled Persons Act 1970 extended the provisions, under the National Assistance Act, for the disabled and made these a duty. In the same year the Local Authority Social Services Act reallocated the provision of home help and laundry services to social services committees.

DOMICILIARY SERVICES

In a broad sense the term domiciliary services can be taken to refer to those services which are specifically aimed at keeping people in their own homes. The term will therefore include the provision of assistance in luncheon clubs, day centres, day hospitals and other establishments outside the actual home, as well as services within the old person's house.

Home helps Permitted under the original legislation and, after 1965, a duty covering the range of elderly and disabled, the Home Help Service has been the responsibility of local authority Social Services Departments since April 1971.

The development of the Home Help Service was hampered by the same factors that slowed down the growth of all the other services: lack of money, lack of legislation and lack of staff (Sumner and Smith, 1969). The lack of staff is often a problem, and the inadequacy of training and promotion opportunities may be contributory aspects of this difficulty. The development of services has been largely left to the discretion of individual organisers and a national pattern of training, promotion prospects and variety of work is essential (Parker and Fish, 1971).

To be a home help involves going into an old person's home and becoming a vital part of his everyday life. In a situation of enforced personal dependency the home help will often build up a very close, supportive relationship with the old person. This relationship has been little used by social workers. Greater flexibility and guidance in the appropriate use of home helps and the information they acquire could bring unexpected benefits.

Home helps have an important role in the prevention of breakdown in the elderly, in supporting older people, in identifying problem situations as they begin to occur, and in reporting back to social workers when breakdown seems likely. While providing care for the ill, disabled, lonely and homebound, home helps do build up close, mutually satisfying relationships, and the elderly people will often have already given their home helps the information a social worker needs. The retrieval and storing of this information could reduce the number of crises and the demands on social workers by pointing to difficulties in their early stages. A visit by the social worker is, after all, a duplication of Social Services Department involvement if a home help is already attending. Some of this duplication ought to be avoidable, to the client's benefit, with better communication between social workers and home helps. A minimum of education on how to see trouble arising and encouraging reporting back should be enough.

One issue arising from this is the problem of confidentiality: the old person may be giving information to the home help because she is seen as a friend (or mother) rather than the agent of a department. In the real situation, however, she is an agent of a department and the information is therefore given to the department, through her, and may be used for the client's benefit.

The Home Help Service has an important part to play in after-care: 'A more generous allocation of help on discharge from hospital for the aged living alone with no relative nearby, would not only assist rehabilitation back into the community, but prevent relapse and possible return to hospital or emergency admittance to welfare homes' (Keay, 1971). The Home Help Service underpins the rest of the community service to the elderly and is the domiciliary service that is most commonly experienced by old people. The information that is gathered through home help contacts can be much more effectively used by social workers in planning for treatment and in implementing plans for helping.

Provision of meals After a spasmodic and sometimes sparse provision of meals services through voluntary organisations, in the 1950s, the government gave local authorities power to provide meals themselves under the National Assistance Act 1948 (Amendment) Act in 1962. In 1971, however, a striking difference in rates of provision between local authority areas was still reported (Stanton, 1970).

A meals service can only be valuable if it is provided sufficiently often and is of sufficient nutritive value to make a significant contribution to the total consumption of the individual old person. This is sometimes complicated by the reluctance, and occasionally, the point-blank refusal of some old people to eat the meals. Some people do have genuine reason to complain about the standard of the meals they receive—or refuse to receive. Others find difficulty in eating them because of ill-fitting false teeth, etc. Sometimes the refusal to eat is an expression of unhappiness and can be seen as a regressive behaviour pattern. Battles over food-intake are a common expression of hostility, anxiety, confusion, etc. in very young children. Oral regressive patterns in old people will sometimes be expressing similar feelings.

This amply illustrates the need, in using resources, for overall co-ordination and planning: the team approach is vital. It is no good sending an old person into hospital to be treated for nutritional deficiencies if he goes home to the same deprived environment. Similarly there is no point arranging for meals-on-wheels to be laid on if he is likely to refuse to eat them when they are delivered. A many-sided approach is essential to cope with a many-sided problem: it may be enough to arrange for a home help to be present at lunchtime for a few days to encourage the old person to eat. It may, at the other extreme, require long-term casework intervention to help him to cope with his fears and anxieties.

One, more recent, development has been the provision of luncheon clubs: these have the advantage of offering social contact as well as nutritional input.

Other local authority schemes The general point applicable to the use of all schemes designed to help keep old people in their homes is that in using them they should be seen as making a contribution to the client's abilities to continue a satisfying process of life. Services are not an end in themselves.

The development of laundry services, chiropody, holiday schemes, sheltered workshops, boarding-out schemes, advisory clinics, etc. has been of variable quality and quantity throughout the country. Whether they are used to make a contribution to the overall plan for helping will depend on local circumstances, on how the individual elderly client feels towards them, and on how the social worker sees them as linking in with other services for the benefit of the individual.

Day centres and day hospitals It is important to make a distinction between social centres and day hospitals: both merit a special mention because of the increasing part they play in providing help for the elderly. A day hospital can be defined as 'a building to which patients may come, or be brought, in the morning, where they may spend several hours in therapeutic activity and whence they return subsequently on the same day to their own homes. ... Day Centres provide social facilities—company, a cooked meal, possibly a bath and chiropody, but none of the remedial services found in the day hospital' (Brocklehurst, 1970).

One role of day hospitals is their contribution to linking the hospital to the community in the minds of the consumers. The hospital has been seen, in the past, as 'the end of the line' for the elderly patient but increased turn-over in hospitals plus the extension of day-time treatment and out-patient clinics are helping to change this image. The role of day care in the care of elderly people is important and fast-expanding. If an old person can be cared for one afternoon a week while her daughter does the shopping this will reduce stress. Many families do not get out of the house together for years on end because someone always has to stay with an old person: an occasional holiday or day out will do much to reduce the danger of breakdown.

One problem has already been alluded to (Mr and Mrs O): patients who attend day hospitals may become involved in a conflict between family and day hospital staff even to the detriment of rehabilitation. A further problem is that those who are most at risk in the community are the single and widowed elderly who live alone. If they are taken to a day centre or hospital, they will have to return to a cold, empty house, usually at the end of a long, cold drive. The most at risk, therefore, can often not be helped by day care—unless additional help can be mobilised: a friend or neighbour to light a fire and switch on the light will make day care much more feasible.

Another problem that sometimes arises is that the day hospital will discharge patients who have come to the end of their treatment back to families who have adjusted to being without them on particular days. To smooth the discharge process relatives can be invited to the day hospital to participate in care, learn about treatment, and plan for the future. Support can be given through discussion between relatives who are caring for elderly patients in their own homes: sharing problems and solutions will bring mutual relief.

In isolation from each other domiciliary resources are often inadequate. Used in planned and co-ordinated ways they can provide a valuable addition to the social work treatment approach. One final word of warning is provided by Shaw's review of services in Sheffield (1971). He suggests that an emphasis on domiciliary services, while important in a community context, may lead to ignoring the more important provision of suitable accommodation and sometimes results in extreme neglect of elderly individuals:

'I regard the failure to provide enough of the proper types of housing for old people as the most serious gap in our statutory services for the old.'

HOUSING

As with other services the progress of housing services was restricted by rationing and shortage of building materials in the post-war years. In the early 1950s some authorities were able to develop sheltered housing schemes. After 1958 the power of welfare authorities to contribute to such schemes was no longer subject to ministerial approval and a steady growth in provision has followed. Housing associations have been encouraged since 1957 when local authorities were given permissive powers to assist associations and a significant contribution has been made to the provision of housing for the elderly since then.

Many old people experience accommodation problems (*Age Concern*, 1973) and those who seek help from statutory agencies frequently do so because of lack of suitable accommodation (A. Harris, 1968; Goldberg, Mortimer and Williams, 1970; Wager, 1972). Sheltered housing, with a warden on call who can give practical help in emergencies, has a major part to play in offsetting these accommodation problems. The warden will be someone, in the future, whose competence, skills and insight should be such as to enable employing authorities to rely on her to diagnose when, and for whom, supervision will be necessary (Willcocks, 1973). Looking at the needs of people in grouped dwellings will involve establishing how far independence is fostered. If this fostering is achieved then there is also a need to explore the nature of its relationship to the ways of meeting the individual's care requirements as arising from his dependency (Boldy, Abel and Carter, 1973).

Housing-needs go beyond the provision of grouped dwelling schemes. Some old people would prefer to remain in their previous home, often the one they have lived in for 60 years, with friends all around. Adapting the existing accommodation with a few handrails, downstairs bathroom, or lavatory, etc. may be a better alternative for some.

The social worker may be involved in making decisions about housing-needs and should remember that a brightly painted, purpose-built home may not be a compensation for the loss of friends and a 'safe', known environment—even if it was materially inadequate.

RESIDENTIAL CARE

In considering residential care, and its use in the care of the elderly, it is important to remember the links between ageing and early life. It is entirely appropriate to apply many of the considerations that have been described and discussed in relation to the use of residential care for children to the needs of the elderly.

Some of the central issues for the field worker in the use of residential care are:

How does it feel to be admitted to a home or residential institution?

How does it feel to admit someone to care?

How does it feel to live in a residential situation?

How does it feel to work in a residential setting?

How does it feel to work with those who work in residential settings?

The need for care   People are admitted to residential care for two basic reasons. They may be admitted for their own protection and included in this approach are concepts of care, treatment, and rehabilitation. At the other extreme they may be admitted for the protection of others and this will include concepts of custody, containment, and again, rehabilitation. Most admissions contain elements of each of these extremes. Goffman (1961) lists five groupings of 'total institutions': (i) those established to care for persons felt to be both incapable and harmless (blind, aged, orphaned); (ii) those established to care for persons felt to be incapable of looking after themselves but presenting a threat to the community (T.B. sanitaria, psychiatric hospitals); (iii) those organised to protect the community against international threat (prisons, concentration camps); (iv) those established to pursue a work-like task (ships, boarding schools); and (v) those designed as retreats from the world (monasteries, convents).

One implication of this approach is that there is unity of aims but this is certainly not so. The expectations of the patient/resident/inmate may differ from those of the staff of the unit, which may differ from the aims of their employing authority, which may differ from the aims of the community. The possibilities for conflict, or collusion, exist all along the line.

A common resort of social workers, especially in local authority Social Services Departments, has been the setting up of waiting lists for old people's homes. To some extent these are realistically an expression of the lack of resources in terms of the total demand. Often they express more than this. It is easy to put people on a waiting list and then forget about them; because of this waiting lists for hospitals or residential care for old people often build up to unrealistic lengths. It is inappropriate to call a group of clients a 'waiting list' and often this is done not as a way of meeting the clients' needs but as a way of reducing pressure on the social worker. To call a halt to community and family pressures for the admission of an old person to care is difficult and causes strains for the worker. This is, however, the only way to find a satisfactory solution to the real problem. A full, careful assessment of the needs of the elderly client is essential before realistic waiting lists show the true need.

Of course some people do present situations of social emergency that require urgent, often immediate action. Others are put on waiting lists because resources are unimaginatively used—the social worker can't think of anything else to do. Others again want (and have a right?) to put their names on a waiting list as insurance against the future.

Interestingly enough, by far the greatest proportion of older people applying for admission to care do so overtly because of the lack of appropriate accommodation (Wager, 1972) and see an old people's home as a solution to this aspect of their lives. Seeing admission in such practical terms, they may be unprepared for the emotional upheaval that is involved.

Admission to care   The conflict of aims which exists in the way residential care is seen—as care, or containment—exists also in the social worker. Anxiety may result from the confusion and guilt about his own motivations and may create problems for the worker. This may be one of the reasons for the emphasis on formal procedures for admission, filling in forms, etc., and pushing responsibility upwards through a hierarchy. These reactions are common to both the admission of children and of old people and in the case of the latter it is not unusual for social workers also to cut off their contact with clients at the point of admission. This may be a reaction to the nature of residential situations and anxiety at having to admit someone but will have an adverse effect on the client in emphasising the rejection of the total community.

Another difficulty for the social worker is the authority content in the admission situation. Removing a child to care, admitting a psychiatrically-ill person compulsorily, and awarding or withholding a vacancy in an old people's home all contain elements of power. Using this power will often present the worker with conflict. Other anxieties may be aroused at having to hand over a client to another worker at the time of admission. Protective feelings—

the 'Whose child is this?' conflict—may be aroused at even partly handing over a client.

From the clients' points of view the way they leave the community, and the way they enter the home, are vital considerations emphasising or reducing the feelings of rejection and acceptance. Meacher (1972) suggests that some residents arrive at old people's homes having been 'taken for a ride' by car or train and find themselves dumped, without explanation, in a home they have never seen. If they have never been out of the house for months, or years, and are a little hard of hearing, or have poor vision, they may be even more confused. Taken out of the house with a minimum of explanation, put in a car and unable to see beyond the window, taken through unfamiliar housing estates or countryside, there is little wonder that they are bewildered and are unable to cope with admission.

This may exaggerate the position and hopefully doesn't apply to many admissions but it is important that full explanations of where they are going are given clearly before admission. Wherever possible, older people should be taken to spend at least a few hours in the home to meet the staff and residents and to understand where and why they are going before the actual admission.

Entering any new group is difficult and small points take on exaggerated importance. Which room to sit in, where to sit for dinner, and which armchair to use are all very important to the individual and planning and preparation can avoid a lot of minor friction and make joining the group easier. The physical appearance of the newly admitted client should not be neglected. If elderly people are being admitted from isolated, withdrawn, and often dirty circumstances efforts should be made to tidy them up: 'She's all right now but you should have seen the state she was in when they first brought her' is heard much too often. This can be prevented with a little care and foresight: if the old person is embarrassed about her clothes no amount of 'smoothing the way' will help.

People in homes   In his generalised consideration of enclosed living Goffman (1961) describes total institutions as characterised by barriers to social intercourse with the outside and the breaking down of barriers between essential living activities (eating, sleeping, daily living, etc.) within. In this sense old people's homes are as much total institutions as prisons. There are, in fact, many prison-like aspects about long-term institutional care for the elderly in physical terms.

In the traditional medical model of caring situations treatment and rehabilitation are the central issues and it is possible to talk of using old people's homes for social rehabilitation. I shall return to this possibility later.

A rather generalised approach is to see the patients or residents as liking being in a custodial or protected situation and seeking to perpetuate their situation by appearing to be ill, or more dependent. This will also be discussed more fully in relation to elderly patients in long-stay hospitals.

Four general problem areas have been identified (Hanson, 1972) as tending to occur to some extent in all total institutions.

(i) *Block treatment* is typified by residents getting up at the same time every day and doing things in 'conveyor-belt' fashion, largely in relation to staff convenience.

(ii) *Regimentation* follows on from block treatment and is typified by a daily routine.

(iii) *Depersonalisation* is another risk when responsibilities are taken away from residents.

(iv) *Social distance* is typified by the absence of conversation except for that which is initiated by the staff. Residents tend not to talk directly to each other but to communicate only with, or through, members of staff.

As far as the whole institution is concerned, then, residents are likely to be compelled by groups and institutional homes to do things in the same way, at the same time every day. This leads in part, to depersonalisation—of which calling old people 'granny' or 'dad' or even by their first names is common evidence. The loss of status and self-esteem that accompanies this leads to ritualisation, often to withdrawal and apathy, and consequently to lack of communication. As far as the individual is concerned there are a variety of ways of reacting to being in an institution: difficult behaviour and childishness are as much expressions of unhappiness as withdrawal and apathy.

The elderly person joins the residential group with a lifetime of experiences and personal contributions to make to the group. When he is admitted he will almost invariably be in a state of personal crisis and will have a confusion of needs. He will have left his own home, furniture, and to a large extent his identity. He will have been deprived of roles and status, being no longer a tenant, payer of the milkman, butcher or baker. He brings with him the need to re-establish roles and to influence and affect others to rebuild self-esteem to preserve self-identity: he also brings the conflict between the need to feel secure and protected and the need to remain an independent, individual person.

Residential workers It has often been suggested that conflict

91

between those goals of the institution that satisfy the needs of the individual and those goals that satisfy the needs of society is inevitable. This external conflict of treatment versus custody may be drawn into the institution and become a conflict between the needs of staff members and the needs of the residents. Menzies (1961) saw the development of the social system in the institution as a defence against anxiety. She studied the nurse-patient relationships and emphasised the splitting up of relationships, depersonalisation, detachment and denial, ritualisation rather than decision-making, the passing upwards of responsibility, and an avoidance of change. Through these mechanisms the nurse is able to put barriers between herself and the pain of becoming too closely involved with the patient.

Staff in old people's homes will tend to fear involvement in interpersonal relationships with elderly residents. The inevitable ending of all relationships in this context, either through death or transfer to hospital, is one real barrier. The transference and counter-transference elements in relationships built up in physically close, dependency situations will involve the arousal of old, complex feelings and these may cause difficulties. Ritualisation and stand-ardisation of task performance avoids the need for constant decision-making and the attendant fear of making the wrong decision.

More positively the residential worker must be concerned prim-arily with the needs of the group within the residential unit. This will mean first of all helping the new member to deal with a new situation. If possible it is sometimes valuable for the residential worker to visit the old person in his own home. This gives both of them the chance to assess each other and the old person an oppor-tunity to show his whole personality on his own ground.

Exploring possible roles within the group and achieving socialisa-tion within the unit can be facilitated for the new resident. Each home has its own set of rules and standards and the residential staff can help to see the rules are explained at the right time. Each indivi-dual has his own background of experiences to offer to the group and if staff can identify areas of common experience among resi-dents these can be built upon to foster new patterns of group relationships.

Another role for the residential worker is recognising the need for old people to contrive to progress along the ageing continuum. Many old people have lived for fifteen years or more in residential care: this is a large slice out of anyone's life and no one will remain static for so long a time. Providing an environment in which personal independence can be maintained and self-direction allowed through decision-making and participation, allows the possibility of growth and change for old people in residential care.

Probably the most important part of caring for old people in a home is providing a warm, protecting, and controlling background. This will involve basic physical care, and the attendant consideration of dependence and independence. It will also mean the provision of a secure foundation from which to view and review the outside world. The controlled use of authority will be a part of every relationship and the way the residential worker handles this will have an important effect on behaviour in the individual and in the whole group. Supporting each individual through protection from scapegoating, providing opportunities for reflection and expression of feelings, helping towards understanding the present and future situation, encouraging and valuing reminiscence, and talking about death are also essential.

To be able to reach an understanding of the group situation and of each individual the residential worker must be able to observe and understand and to communicate the understanding and an acceptance of the individual. There is also a need to retain and foster community links. Offsetting role-loss is one objective but more generally the old people's home can be opened up and the institutional pressures reduced by bringing in the outside, everyday world.

In fulfilling these tasks the residential worker in the old people's home faces some real difficulties in the living situation. Demands are made on the individual living in the home in the form of intrusions on the lives of married couples living in, and in hindering the single worker in developing and maintaining outside contacts. In addition, shift work and living in mean physical stress and long hours.

Residential worker and field worker Communication between field and residential workers is essential if both are to get a complete picture of the resident and learn to deal with the whole person. One danger is the labelling of a resident, representing the failure to see him as a whole person. The residential worker may see the old person all day, every day, but this very closeness may make it difficult for him to see objectively the needs that the older person may express. Similarly the field worker may assess more objectively but miss a lot of information and opportunities for relating to the client.

It is also necessary for workers to communicate in order to facilitate admission and discharge procedures for the old person and continued contact between field worker and client brings wider opportunities for him to extend contacts into the community. The field worker can also offer supportive help to the residential worker

—and vice versa—through clarification, expression of feeling, etc. The breakdown of communication results partly from the genuine difference between the contexts in which they work and from the 'Whose child is this?' conflict. It may also result from a real or imagined difference of status: residential work is a less well-paid job and training is, so far, less extensive than for field workers. This is especially true of work with the elderly.

Social rehabilitation and residential care Most old people go into homes because there is no real accommodation alternative, and people who are being admitted to homes are increasingly frail. Some people, however, deteriorate in their own homes because of loneliness, isolation, and lack of food, warmth and companionship. These people are admitted to homes in a poor state of health and morale and after some months of care, good food, and company they are well enough to return home. At present they are usually expected to sell their houses and give up furniture soon after admission. If these escape routes and exits can be kept open for longer then a few more people could be returned from residential care to their own homes.

If social workers stop seeing residential homes for the elderly as no more than ante-rooms to death and begin to see them as places in which change and growth can take place then old people's homes could realistically begin to be used for social rehabilitation in the same way as hospitals are seen as providing medical rehabilitation. This is not to advocate a descent on homes to uproot settled and content old people but it is a proposal for more thought and care in admission and different expectations of care on the part of both worker and elderly client. This implies continuing contact with the old person after admission and regular reviews. No child would be allowed to go into a home and be forgotten: the same must apply to old people.

Old people's homes have an important role in providing short-term care. In very short-term situations of family crisis, family holidays, or in longer-term situations of three to six months during illness, or while families move house, etc., short-term care can be very important. Two weeks' holiday a year can reduce stress and allow families to cope for the rest of the year. Care during the winter months may help an old person cope alone for the summer months. The important point is, once again, flexibility.

THE ELDERLY PATIENT

Not all the elderly sick are cared for by the specialist in geriatric medicine. Many older people are treated in acute beds by specialists in various branches of medicine. 'However, many elderly people are not cured when treated for their presenting condition, or if they are it may be only for a short time and then they require re-admission. These patients demand the attention of a specialist doctor in their own right. Their care is frequently complicated by considerable disability and frailty which may be due to multiple disease processes as well as old age' (Hall, 1973). This partly accounts for the growth of geriatric medicine.

Appropriate hospital care for the elderly patient demands the same as appropriate social work care for the elderly client—a full assessment that will take account of the multiplicity and complexity of symptoms. The first requirement is, therefore, a full assessment of the need for treatment. Only after this assessment has been made can arrangements for return home or transfer to a long-stay bed be arranged. Hospital accommodation should be viewed in totality and each patient should be in the right place for his individual needs at any one point in time.

Reactions to the institution It is not always possible to offer appropriate care and in the past many old people have become stuck in institutions, unable to get out, and condemned to long-term 'imprisonment'. The enforced institutional situation with the problems that have already been described, of depersonalisation, ritualisation, authoritarianism, etc., have often led to institutional neurosis (Barton, 1959). The patient becomes apathetic and withdrawn; over-dependence, lack of initiative, and typically disinterested posture and expression are common.

Over-protection of patients is a reaction partly to fear of them and what may happen if they are not controlled, and partly to the fear of the pain that goes with becoming involved in close interpersonal relationships. Nurses may sometimes encourage dependency to meet their own needs. Whitehead (1970) suggests three factors which tend to perpetuate these undesirable trends: the lack of satisfactorily motivated staff, poorly trained staff who are unaware of the basic emotional needs of the elderly, and an authoritarian regime productive of petty restrictions and staff fears. It is worth speculating on how far the patients' own needs to perpetuate a protective environment could be added to this list.

Reactions to enforced physical dependency take many forms. For some patients a denial of the reality is one way of coping: in its extreme form this may involve seeing the hospital as a hotel and demanding hotel service. Withdrawal and aggressive behaviour are both ways of reacting to the same external threat to individuality. For others the response can be a total submersion in childlike dependency on nursing and medical staff. Most seem to achieve an uneasy pretence that the 'pains of imprisonment' are an acceptable price to pay for care. There is no doubt that many patients in long-stay hospitals achieve a kind of satisfaction in life in spite of the many restrictions. For some this is a pretence and any attempt to change their lives presents them with the reality and consequent unhappiness. For others the satisfaction is genuine and perhaps some people like hospitals because they meet their dependency-needs. Those who continue to fight illness (and caring services) usually stay in the community; those who seek protection and dependence sometimes gravitate to the hospitals.

The hospital as an organisation Within the hospital there are rules and standards of behaviour and formalised channels of communication. In addition to these formal channels there are also many underlying informal channels of communication and expectations of behaviour. The social system puts its own particular pressures on the elderly patient. The 'good' patient is the one who conforms, who behaves himself, who does not make demands, and who generally subordinates his own personality to the needs of the institution. The 'bad' patient is the one who wants his morning coffee at 11.30, instead of 10.30, the one who makes his presence felt through continual demands, the one, in other words, who is determined to remain an individual. Great pressures can be put on the latter patient to make him conform: 'We can't cope with his demands and his noise any longer; can't he be transferred to the psycho-geriatric unit?' Presumably the psycho-geriatric unit is expected to teach him to be a good boy.

The social worker's task Traditionally the social worker's role in this kind of situation has been to work with the individual and his reactions to his illness, dependence, and his environment. In working in a long-stay geriatric setting this is not enough. The social worker must approach the problem of the whole organisation, and the way it impinges on the individual living within it. The social worker role on this level should be that of catalyst—a role involving identifying behaviour patterns, communication, and stimulation of action. Work on changing attitudes—education—can be done with individual members of staff and with groups of staff, of patients, and of relatives. The objective is the creation of a place in which people can live, not a place in which bodies are stored and kept clean and well fed.

The results of failure of communication can be illustrated:

Mrs U (69) was admitted to hospital following a cardio-vascular accident in July and was transferred to the geriatric admission ward the following January. She came to the notice of the social worker in March.

When the social worker first visited she was taken to where Mrs U was sitting in the day room by the sister who merely pointed and said, 'That's her.'

'I sat down beside Mrs U who impressed as a rather unhappy, depressed person who was dejected and rather forlorn: quite unable to look ahead. Her transfer to the geriatric ward had given no encouragement or incentive, Mrs U being so aware of the fact that most of the other patients were very much older and quite incapable of holding a conversation with her.'

The social worker noticed that the staff on duty were irritable with the patients and one nurse turned to the social worker, thinking she was a visitor, and said, 'And you shouldn't be here either, it isn't visiting time.'

'Mrs U spoke nostalgically about her happy home life, her relatives, friends and neighbours who visited regularly and in particular about her husband who came every evening and twice daily at weekends. Although he worked full-time Mrs U suggested her husband would give up his employment to look after her if she was considered fit for discharge.

Mrs U referred to letter-writing activities as her only occupation each day—she had been waiting many weeks for a caliper and then she could practise walking again. She was being offered no stimulus within the hospital and appeared to be treated as senile. Despite this she was clear-thinking and alert.'

The social worker felt Mrs U would be quite suitable for rehabilitation at a day hospital and decided to press for Mrs U's discharge with day hospital care. Mr U was seen at home and the position fully discussed with him. He confirmed that he was willing to give up his job if she was discharged and was able and willing to carry out alterations to the home. There had been no communication whatsoever between Mr U and the medical staff—he had assumed that he would be told when his wife was ready for

discharge: 'When you take your watch to be mended
you leave it in the hands of the expert and you trust him—
I thought it was the same in hospital.'

These facts were reported to the consultant who agreed
to her discharge with attendance three days a week at
the day hospital. The sister-in-charge was reluctant to agree
and made no attempt to help: she suggested the social
worker should bring Mr U to the hospital early one morning
to see how difficult his wife really was. Mr U had not
been forceful or demanding but had accepted his wife's
treatment unquestioningly. She had received little
stimulation, apparently because she had been labelled as
'undeserving' or 'difficult' by nursing staff.

At the beginning of April Mrs U was discharged and when
the social worker visited the following week she reported:

'Mr U had already obtained a wheel-chair and had taken
his wife to the hairdresser. (Mrs U later said her hair had
only been washed twice in hospital and then it had been
done in the bath.)'

She improved rapidly at home and with help from the day
hospital where she received treatment from physiotherapists
and occupational therapists. The individual attention re-
established her self-respect and within a week of being
home she 'looked a different person'.

Mrs U was ignored and forgotten on the ward and had the
social worker not intervened the patient may have
been unable to continue to withstand the rejection and have
withdrawn into herself—acting out the role demanded
by the staff.

Using casework techniques to help elderly patients is one way
of offering social work help. Approaching the problem from the
other end—by treating the institution rather than the individual—
will also be an essential part of social work in a long-stay geriatric
hospital. Using groups to promote understanding, communication,
and change will certainly arouse hostility and anxieties in the short
run but will help to create a more enlightened hospital in the
long run.

'The psycho-geriatric problem'   Old people over the age of 65 make
up the largest group of long-stay patients in mental illness hospitals:
there are about 76,000 long-stay patients and of these 36,000 are
over 65 years old. Not only this but about 44 per cent of patients
in psychiatric hospitals are over 65 and more than half of these

(27,000) are over 75. 'These are the people who are at the mercy of a society in which only the strongest can survive and flourish. No politician canvasses their votes; no advertiser sees them as a target audience; no television producer would shape a programme to stimulate their interest. They are worked out, thrown out, superfluous and forgotten' (Mind Report, 1972).

A few months after this emotive appeal the Department of Health and Social Security (October, 1972) laid down new guidelines for hospital services for mental illness related to old age. For those patients who have grown old in mental hospitals it was recommended that no new accommodation should be provided but that accommodation should be improved. For other elderly patients suffering from psycho-pathological change it laid down comprehensive guidelines for the provision of care and accommodation.

There is, as yet, a disturbing lack of total help and understanding of the 'psycho-geriatric problem'. The social work contribution has been minimal and usually restricted to containment rather than treatment. Certainly casework techniques have yet to be proved to have anything to offer in the treatment of dementia but conditions of care can still be improved tremendously and social workers can contribute to this improvement. The conditions exposed by *Sans Everything* (Robb, 1967) still exist.

COMMUNITY CARE

The term 'community care' is frequently used to describe the services that are provided in the community rather than the care and support already being given by the community. A total view of community care will mean considering society at four levels: 'the client and his family; the social network of the family; kin, friends, and neighbours; the social worker and other local authority workers and services; and some form of residential care' (Bayley, 1973).

The care of old people in the community is still provided mainly by families but many additional services have been provided by voluntary effort. A tremendous range and variety of services are provided, particularly through voluntary old people's welfare committees, although development is patchy and has been spasmodic. Clubs, meals services, visiting services, transport, fund-raising, holidays, library services, running errands, home decorating, have all relied heavily on voluntary efforts.

Community development approach   One report of a development project (Cheeseman, Lansley and Wilson, 1972) has described the possibilities of setting up neighbourhood care groups. This approach is designed not just to ask people what they want but to go further and involve the people in providing the service they need. The worker is then not in the client-caseworker relationship but is working alongside people as a colleague and a friend.

The development of neighbourhood schemes is one way to attack the problems that really concern people in their own locality. Encouraging the care of elderly people as part of the overall development of a neighbourhood is important in avoiding the segregation of older people from care. An additional advantage of this approach is that it is possible to involve voluntary workers from the local area who would never have taken part in traditionally organised voluntary groups.

Voluntary visiting Visiting services have been established with different objectives in mind and have developed in two main ways. One approach has been the careful selection of visitor and elderly person to match them as people in an attempt to establish a close friendly relationship. The second approach has been designed to reach all lonely and housebound old people in an area to establish at least a minimum of contact with them all (NOPWC, 1967).

It has already been suggested that there is an important role for the voluntary visitor in relation to the isolated client. If the professional worker is able, after full assessment, to restore an old person to an adequate level of functioning then a voluntary visitor can often provide the continuing care, support, and contact to keep him functioning at that level. It is, however, important that communication between professional and voluntary workers is on a regular basis so that if things start to deteriorate then this can be recognised and the information passed on.

Boarding-out schemes One of the major problems that faces old people, and those who care for them, is the lack of appropriate accommodation. Voluntary organisations have run a number of boarding-out schemes in a few areas—Bedfordshire Old People's Welfare Council, Cheshire Community Council, Exeter Council of Social Services, and Plymouth Guild of Social Service have all established schemes. Some local authorities—notably Flintshire and Hampshire—have also set up similar schemes (NOPWC, 1969).

Finding people to provide this care requires a lot of effort and the extent and quality of care that can be provided will vary widely. It would be interesting to see an extension of the use of 'foster care' for elderly people, especially by local authority departments. It might be most appropriate in short-term situations, perhaps following discharge from hospital, or during family holidays, etc.

The vast majority of older people continue to be cared for in the community, in the sense that they do not enter long-term institutional care. Most of them remain in contact with their children, if they do not actually live with them. The family remains the basic unit of support within the community and additional services are provided through voluntary agencies to supplement, and sometimes lead the way for, the statutory services.

THE CARING CONTINUUM

It is possible to see the whole of provision of practical care for the elderly as a continuum: each individual older person has a right to be at a point along that continuum which is appropriate to his own particular needs at any one point in time. It has often been suggested that there are not enough resources to permit this ideal situation. There can be little doubt that there are not enough resources but there is also no doubt that the resources that are at present available could be used in better ways. By implication this means greater flexibility.

It should not be assumed that all old people are better off, or happier in their own homes: for some a residential home may be therapeutic or at least more satisfactory than a lonely, isolated existence in a cold, deteriorated house, without the money to improve conditions. In the long run this is an argument for better housing, better domiciliary services, and bigger pensions. In the short run the real-life situation is that some old people need institutional care.

The demand for institutional resources may be seen in terms of a funnelling of needs: too many needs are being crammed into the funnel. There are at least three ways of reducing the pressures at the mouth of the funnel and ensuring that nobody is squeezed out.

The most obvious way of reducing pressure on resources would be by increasing the total provision. One problem of this approach is that there is a degree of unmet demand that emerges when new homes are established. Local communities seem able to cope with the elderly among them until a home is built and then demands begin to be made.

A second way of reducing the demand for residential care is by increasing the use of domiciliary resources. If this is to be effective then services should be injected before breakdown, rather than at crisis point. Identifying those people who are at risk and who are likely to need help is therefore a priority in the proper use of resources in the elderly person's home.

The most unexplored method of reducing pressure on the whole of the caring provision for the elderly is the use of residential care to provide therapy. People can be helped back to a reasonable, satisfying life at home and maintained at pre-crisis level with short-term, intensive treatment. This treatment could well include a short period in an old people's home. This requires a change in attitude towards the use of residential care on the part of workers inside as well as outside the homes. As long as present attitudes prevail, death is the only way out of homes and those who are waiting are effectively waiting to step into 'dead men's shoes'. This places additional strain on residential workers who on the one hand are expected—and usually want—to provide care and protection, and on the other hand feel under pressure to create vacancies for those who are waiting.

A further block to providing appropriate care within the institution system is the administrative division between hospitals and local authority homes. One problem that results from the split is a kind of 'body-bartering' : old people will only be transferred from hospital to home if they can be exchanged, and vice versa. Sometimes, especially in a country area, this means an old person has to move to a home up to twenty or thirty miles from his home and friends. The only way to achieve treatment for the whole person is by striving to remove this barrier and to provide continuity of care. There should be an overview of the continuum of care so that each old person can receive services appropriate to his individual needs.

Using practical help to the best advantage for all will, therefore, involve a knowledge of local resources both generally and individually. A total assessment of the needs of the individual will lead to an understanding of the right help for his needs in terms of what is realistically available. Meeting those needs through the development of a helping relationship and the provision of practical aid is the fundamental social work task.

7

Conclusions

A spate of surveys by independent bodies, voluntary agencies, local authorities and government departments has amply indicated the extent of the unmet need for services that exists in the field of the care of the elderly. Most services could be increased considerably and still be in arrears of demand.

It is not within the scope of this book to examine in detail the policies and planning needed to cope with this unmet need. An extremely good survey of policy and planning issues in local authority services already exists (Sumner and Smith, 1969). It is important, however, to examine a number of other issues in the social work care of ageing people in so far as they have an immediate bearing on the direction of social work. Especially significant are aspects of evaluation, prevention, and education.

EVALUATION

Until very recently, little work had been done on the measurement of techniques used by social workers or on the assessment of change that takes place as a result of social work intervention.

The usefulness of evaluation of effectiveness is obvious: realistic planning for individual and agency resources cannot take place without an understanding of the consequences of resource allocation. The study of social work effectiveness carried out by Goldberg and others between 1965 and 1970 is an extremely valuable contribution to understanding social work and the elderly client. This study also has much wider implications for the assessment of social work in many different settings.

The field of old age was chosen for the study for several reasons: the increasing challenge of community care for the elderly; the unique staffing conditions in the field at the time; and the possibilities for quantifying work with the elderly because much of the help, they felt, would be of a practical kind. The target of the study was to assess the social and medical condition of 300 old people referred to the welfare department of a London borough. On referral the clients were allocated randomly but equally to a special group who were to receive help from trained social workers and a comparison group who would be in the care of the department's social welfare officers.

The social and medical condition and needs of each client were assessed by a social worker and a physician on referral, and again 10½ months later. The clients tended to be more incapacitated than similar samples: a quarter suffered from disease severe enough to constitute a threat to life and 15 per cent suffered from psychiatric disorders. Although half were already receiving some personal social services at the time of referral, many additional needs were found: only about 5 per cent required residential care.

The amount and quality of the social work provided in each group differed greatly. The old people in the special group received more attention because the trained social workers had smaller caseloads. The trained workers saw more problems and put more emphasis on casework and on help for relatives. Both groups had significantly fewer practical needs after reassessment but the clients in the special group felt more satisfied with life, were more active, less depressed, and had fewer worries than those in the comparison group. A reduction in practical needs in both groups was related to input, in terms of numbers of contacts and items of practical help given. It was not possible, however, to identify precisely the elements in the casework process which were responsible for changes in attitude and feelings.

Trained social workers, then, did not bring any extra change in physical circumstances but did create a general improvement of morale in relation to attitudes and feelings about those physical circumstances.

These results have some implications for the social work task: (a) the greater importance of environmental and practical support in working with this age group; (b) the need to reach out and hold frail, and physically and mentally handicapped clients; (c) the need to protect elderly clients, as with children, from the neglect or apathy of others but recognising the difficulties of going too far into over-protection; (d) the need for the social worker to act as an enabler in recognising needs and helping clients accept services; (e) the need for a careful and sound initial assessment; and (f) the need for special casework skills: awareness of a slower pace, of loss and depression, of restrictions in life-space, and of difficulties in absorbing new experiences; an awareness of casework as being less concerned with adjusting maladaptive behaviour and more with the provision of environmental supports; and an awareness of the relevance of transference and counter-transference in working with older people.

This study serves to emphasise, in the real-life context, many of the aspects of working with the ageing client that have already been discussed at length. A further important study was conducted, also by Goldberg, with Neill (1972) in a medical general practice and some aspects of this are relevant to work with older people. This study set out broadly to examine the nature of problems presented in a general practice in Camden, what expectations doctors and patients had of social workers, and how social work could most effectively be organised and presented.

Over a third of the 1,000 patients referred over four years were elderly, and material needs predominated among these elderly people. However, the type of social work action, assessment, casework, or referral elsewhere, was not found to vary markedly with clients' age. The study concluded that the elderly clearly demand attention from social workers, whether they work in local authority or general practice. The needs of frail, old people for a variety of domiciliary services and better material living conditions were demonstrated in this project, as they have been by numerous other studies. Old people, it was suggested, who are facing problems in family and interpersonal situations and also painful post-retirement adjustments are in need of casework skills which are often in short supply and used for younger people.

Once again the need to examine fully the total requirements of elderly clients is emphasised and the current distribution of skills and resources in social services is questioned.

Most elderly clients examined by both of these studies expressed material needs. Presenting appropriate resources after referral is one way of handling the needs. A more suitable method of helping, in the long run, might be to identify individuals at risk to prevent collapse, and to make wider social provisions to reduce risk.

PREVENTION

The need to identify old people who are at risk in the community has been well recognised. Some groups of older people are particularly at risk and these might be listed as follows:

(i) The physically incapacitated: those who are housebound or who are severely restricted in their capacity to maintain personal care are particularly vulnerable. Personal care will include the ability to carry out basic physical tasks in order to keep an independent home running and to provide the basic needs of life, especially food, warmth, and clean linen.

(ii) The mentally impaired: those who are forgetful, or confused, psychotic or otherwise mentally infirm will also be at risk.

(iii) The bereaved: those who have suffered recent loss of a significant person in their lives are vulnerable to illness, and even death. This is particularly true of recently widowed old men who are more likely to die than widowed old women.

(iv) The very isolated: those who have few social contacts are likely to be subject to loneliness and deterioration in their physical and environmental circumstances. This group is more likely to include single and widowed old people than those with children, or husband, or wife alive.

(v) The very old.

One way of identifying old people in the community would be by maintaining a total register of all people over a certain age. This information already exists in various scattered forms and, apart from the value of the overall view of need which could be obtained from such a register, this would provide a good foundation for building a preventive service (Meacher, 1970).

One major problem of providing a preventive service is the difficulty of maintaining a valid, up-to-date register. In developing a register of the elderly who are at risk it should be possible to identify a good deal of existing information in health, and social services departments, in hospitals and in housing departments. If the information can be put together in one place by someone with a co-ordinating role, perhaps in a health centre, social services area office, or local hospital, then the next problem will be maintenance of the register.

Many workers are regularly in contact with old people at risk: district nurses, health visitors, social workers, and home helps. If co-ordination of the information that all these workers have can be arranged then maintenance of a register might be possible. Perhaps home helps in particular have the greatest source of currently unused knowledge. Some fundamental problems of confidentiality, privacy, and economics will require to be resolved.

If total needs are identified then better planning for the needs of the elderly as a group is possible. Remedying the social deprivations that older people are subjected to would enable them to meet risk from a sounder basis. The poor housing, lack of money to pay for food and warmth, and general shrinking of social choice that go with old age must all be improved before prevention can be a meaningful concept. Underlying all these necessary changes is the need for different attitudes to the elderly: respect for the dignity of age is lacking and the greatest need of all is for the change in attitudes.

EDUCATION

Changes of attitudes will follow from education at all levels. Our society as a whole has a particular approach to old age that has an immediate and important effect on the health and happiness of old people. On the whole the relationships of families to their elderly members remain good in individual situations but trends of employment, demography, economics, and family development increasingly emphasise the sense of isolation and separateness of individual old people.

A basic problem exists in the altering of community attitudes to the value of old age. An increased understanding of the realities of ageing and of the needs of older people may reduce stress, fears, and anxieties. More research into the circumstances of older people will help with this understanding.

Many older people could play a role in participating in community services. With time and energies to spare, after retirement, voluntary activity is one way of maintaining status and involvement. The more that older people are able to participate in activities that are valued by the community, for their caring if not their economic contribution, then the more those older people will be valued for themselves.

Older people themselves have a right to continuing education. Pre-retirement education is given in the form of teaching on what to expect of the retirement experience and how to use money and leisure. Beyond this, provision for education in leisure is needed. Education is rightly geared to the needs of younger people but greater provision for older age groups will help to maintain interest, activity and involvement, and therefore self-respect.

Professional workers, too, need greater understanding of the needs and behaviour of older people. Training in geriatric medicine is increasingly being extended and education for nurses will hopefully move in close parallel. Social work education must follow suit. The teaching of human growth, behaviour, and development has too often tended to peter out after adolescence. The developmental links between early life and later life need to be spelled out, as well as the normality of age-changes. An understanding of the possible satisfactions and the realistic possibilities for change can be linked to the objectives and possibilities for social work intervention.

Social work for the elderly is possible within particular limitations and with particular extensions to practice with younger people. An over-enthusiastic plea for teaching to demonstrate the joys of working with the elderly is inappropriate here. What is needed is honest understanding and explanation of the needs of ageing people in order to allay the fears, anxieties and pressures that prevent full assessment and treatment.

SUMMARY

Social work provision for ageing clients has too often been based on a stereotyped view—old people only need practical services, like a home help, or meals-on-wheels, or a bath seat, and somebody who can keep a friendly eye on them. The unspoken addition is that the success of social work in this view is the death of the elderly client who can then be removed from the caseload.

This approach is a reflection partly of the general attitude of society and partly of the feelings within the individual. The existence of anxieties about death and physical change in the social worker may make working with older people stressful. In addition to this there are real conflicts in the social circumstances of older people—family stress, environmental stress, and internal stress in the individual. To be caught up in a hostile or depressive situation is unpleasant. Only a minority of social workers express a preference for work with the elderly for these and for many other reasons.

Social work with the elderly should be concerned with offering individual solutions in a flexible way. Each person grows old in his own particular ways and although general trends in normal ageing can be described some characteristic problems can be identified. The interrelationship of social (occupational changes, family changes, changes in the adequacy of social provisions, etc.), medical, and psychiatric problems is a fundamental reason for using a range of professional skills.

The social worker who is faced with an older person in difficulty must begin with an attempt at problem definition. Problems will tend to be presented in terms of the resources that are seen to be available: clients will often define a problem within particular limits and in terms of the solution that they can see. The first task of the social worker is to detach the problem from the resources and take a new look at it. This will involve decisions about who needs to believe that there is a problem in the situation: whether the old person himself feels unhappy, or lonely, or in need of care, or whether others in his immediate environment feel he should be receiving care.

The resources that are available to the social worker will be on two levels: the practical, material resources, and the personal skill of the social worker himself in using and building interpersonal relationships. There will be certain limitations on the development of a relationship between the social worker and his elderly client. The time element plays an important part and moving at the client's pace is essential. Difficulties of communication may demand more patience in developing relationships with older clients. Loss of hearing, sight, or speech sometimes involves the social worker in a greater use and understanding of non-verbal communication. Physical expression becomes more important, as do actions; and silence, too, can become more meaningful. Complications of physical distress and confusion may also exist.

In spite of these difficulties the basic social work task is the establishment of a relationship with the elderly client and the client's relatives or others in the immediate social network. As far as the elderly person himself is concerned the social worker can help him to consider the realities of his current situation and discuss the available alternatives in the present. Beyond this it will be important to help him to see an ongoing pattern in his life. Contentment in the present will depend on an acceptance that what has gone before has been relevant; in part it may also depend on seeing value in the future. In this context reminiscence may have a therapeutic value in itself.

There is often a lot of pressure on children to care for their elderly parent: some will need support in coping with their feelings of guilt at being unable to care (especially as the children of an 80-year-old person may well be middle-aged and beginning to face the idea of death in a personal sense). Recent studies have done much to dispel the myth that children do not care for their aged parents. In reality if stress does exist it is often based on longstanding family conflict. The social worker may have a part to play in alleviating or resolving these conflicts through practical help, discussion, and occasionally through fostering insights into the real basis of difficulties.

The social worker is one link between his clients and the resources they need. He may be directly instrumental in giving or withholding the resources or he may be involved in creating a situation in which the resources can be accepted and used appropriately. In using resources the most important factor will be flexibility. A full assessment will lead to a knowledge of the client's needs that will enable resources to be appropriately applied to the needs of the individual.

PROBLEM, PROCESS AND PATTERN

Care for the elderly fails when it deals with ongoing problems by the application of static solutions. We are all involved in the ageing process and only for a minority will growing old lead to problems that will require help from outside the normal supportive network of family and friends. The need for outside help will usually mean calling not only on the doctor or social worker, but will involve an interrelated team of professionals who are equipped to deal with the multi-symptomatic basis of most of the problems of elderly people. Solutions should aim to deal not just with a limited view of the here-and-now but should be concerned with restoring a normal, ongoing process of growing old, with the satisfactions that this will imply.

The social work contribution should be on many levels. The social worker must build up a relationship with his client that will enable them to explore the real, underlying nature of difficulties, to discuss the available solutions, and to reach out for those solutions in a way that will avoid damage to the client. He should also seek out, with his client, the pattern which the present makes with the past, and the future: ego-integrity depends on perceiving the relevance of the past and the inevitability of death—we must allow people the right to die in their own way. A quality of death is as important as a quality of life. Continual reappraisal of the treatment approach is essential, as is continued liaison with other caring professionals.

A pattern of successful ageing will be seen to grow out of a recognition of the normality of the process and of the fact that problems are only relevant in terms of this process. Resources and helping sevices tend to be emergency-orientated and can be redirected towards preventive work through an increasing consideration of the restoration of normality rather than the application of static solutions without a full understanding of total need.

Suggestions for further reading

Readers of this book will probably be only too aware of the lack of literature that has been written specifically about social work and elderly clients. The problem for the social worker lies in being able to select material from many sources in order to apply it to human need. I have tried to draw together some of the literature in this book and relate it to field practice but information is very scattered.

Field (*The Aged, the Family, and the Community*, 1972) has produced a very interesting book on the needs of older people in the community, although this is directed very much towards the USA. Rudd (*Human Relations in Old Age*, 1967) also offers very useful ideas about relationships and attitudes towards the elderly. The works of Townsend (*The Last Refuge*, 1962) and Meacher (*Taken for a Ride*, 1972) provide valuable understanding of older people in institutional situations, whilst that of Goldberg, Mortimer and Williams (*Helping the Aged*, 1970) has added considerably to the practical evidence of the effectiveness of social work approaches to elderly clients.

The sociological perspectives of ageing have been brought together by Wilson in two review articles ('Old Age', 1973a; 'Old Age, 2', 1973b).

In these papers Wilson looks at British and American literature and additional references are provided. Particularly valuable books are the linked studies of Tunstall (*Old and Alone*, 1966) and Shanas et al. (*Old People in Three Industrial Societies*, 1968). The former is a study of isolation and loneliness and includes a summary of the relevant theoretical approaches; Tunstall's survey goes to make up a part of the larger work, *Old People in Three Industrial Societies*. This examines the needs and circumstances of old people in Britain, Denmark, and the USA, and is certainly essential reading for anyone with an interest in ageing. Townsend's earlier work (*The Family*

Life of Old People, 1963) is also useful reading.

Bromley (*The Psychology of Human Ageing*, 1966) offers a survey of the emotional, psychiatric, and psychological behaviour of the older person. Chown (*Human Ageing*, 1972) gives a collection of papers on psychological aspects of ageing, dealt with under the headings of personality and cognition. Both these books are clear, easily read, and very useful.

A general introduction to the practice of geriatric medicine can be obtained from Agate (*Geriatrics for Nurses and Social Workers*, 1972 and *The Practice of Geriatrics*, 1970). Also very helpful is the basic text produced by Hazell (*Social and Medical Problems of the Elderly*, 1973).

There is an increasing amount being written about death and dying: a useful starting point is Hinton's book, *Dying* (1967).

Bibliography

AGATE, J. (1970), *The Practice of Geriatrics*, Heinemann.

AGATE, J. (1972), *Geriatrics for Nurses and Social Workers*, Heinemann.

AGE CONCERN (1973), *Age Concern on Accommodation*.

BAKER, R. (1972), 'The challenge for British casework', *Social Work Today*, vol. 2, no. 19, 13 January.

BARTON, R. (1959), *Institutional Neurosis*, John Wright.

BAYLEY, M. (1973), *Mental Handicap and Community Care*, Routledge & Kegan Paul.

BLANK, M. L. (1971), 'Recent research findings on practice with the ageing', *Social Casework*, June, pp. 382-8.

BLAU, P. (1967), *Exchange and Power in Social Life*, John Wiley.

BLENKNER, M. (1965), 'Social work and family relationships in later life with some thoughts on filial maturity', in Shanas and Streib (eds), *Social Structure and the Family—Generational Relations*, Prentice-Hall.

BOLDY, D., ABEL, P. and CARTER, K. (1973), 'Profile of the elderly in grouped housing', *Age Concern Today*, no. 7, Autumn.

BOTWINICK, J. (1966), 'Cautiousness with advanced age', *Journal of Gerontology*, vol. 21, pp. 347-53.

BREARLEY, C. P. (1972), 'Waiting for age', *Social Work Today*, vol. 3, no. 18, 14 December.

BROCKLEHURST, J. C. (1970), *The Geriatric Day Hospital*, King Edward's Hospital Fund for London.

BROMLEY, D. B. (1966), *The Psychology of Human Ageing*, Penguin Books.

BUMAGIN, V. E. (1972), 'Challenge of working with old people', *Social Work Today*, vol. 3, no. 18, 14 December.

BUTLER, R. N. (1969), 'Ageism, another form of bigotry', *Gerontologist*, vol. 9, pp. 243-6.

CARTWRIGHT, A., HOCKEY, L. and ANDERSON, J. L. (1973), *Life Before Death*, Routledge & Kegan Paul.

CENTRAL STATISTICAL OFFICE (1972), *Social Trends*, no. 3, HMSO.

CHEESEMAN, D., LANSLEY, J. and WILSON, J. (1972), *Neighbourhood Care and Old People*, Bedford Square Press.

CHOWN, S. M. (1972), *Human Ageing*, Penguin Books.

CRAWFORD, M. (1972), 'Retirement and role-playing', *Sociology*, vol. 6, no. 2, May.

CUMMING, E. and HENRY, W. E. (1961), *Growing Old—The Process of Disengagement*, Basic Books.

DEPARTMENT OF HEALTH AND SOCIAL SECURITY (1972), 'Services for mental illness related to old age', HMSO.

Economic and Financial Problems of the Provision for Old Age (1954), Cmd, 9333, HMSO.

ERIKSON, E. H. (1964), *Childhood and Society*, Norton & Co. Inc. (revised edition).

FIELD, M. (1972), *The Aged, the Family and the Community*, Columbia University Press.

FREUD, S. (1920), *Beyond the Pleasure Principle*, in *The Complete Psychological Works of Sigmund Freud*, ed. J. Strachey, Hogarth Press, 1955 edn.

FREUD, S. (1937), *New Introductory Lectures on Psycho-Analysis*, Hogarth Press.

FRY, M. (1954), *Old Age Looks at Itself*, Churchill Livingstone.

GOFFMAN, E. (1961), *Asylums*, Penguin Books.

GOLDBERG, E. M., MORTIMER, A. and WILLIAMS, B. T. (1970), *Helping the Aged*, NISWT, no. 19, Allen & Unwin.

GOLDBERG, E. M. and NEILL, J. E. (1972), *Social Work in General Practice*, NISWT, no. 23, Allen & Unwin.

GOLDFARB, A. I. (1965), 'Psychodynamics and the three-generation family', in E. Shanas and G. F. Streib (eds), *Social Structure and the Family— Generational Relations*, Prentice-Hall.

GORE, I. Y. (1972), 'Physical activity and ageing—a survey of the Soviet literature', *Geront. Clin.*, vol. 14, no. 2, pp. 65-85.

GORE, I. Y. (1973), *Age and Vitality*, Allen & Unwin.

GREGORY, P. and YOUNG, M. (1972), 'Lifeline telephone service for the elderly', National Innovations Centre.

GULBENKIAN REPORT (1968), *Community Work and Social Change*, report of a study group on training set up by the Calouste Gulbenkian Foundation, Longman.

HALL, M. R. P. (1973), 'A green and smiling age', inaugural lecture, Southampton University.

HANSON, J. (1972), *Residential Care Observed*, NISWT and *Age Concern*.

HARRIS, A. (1968), *Social Welfare for the Elderly*, Government Social Survey carried out on behalf of the NCCOP and the Scottish Home and Health Department.

HARRIS, C. C. (1969), *The Family*, Allen & Unwin.

HAVINGHURST, R. J. (1968), 'Personality and patterns of ageing', *Gerontologist*, vol. 8, pp. 20-3.

HAZELL, K. (1973), *Social and Medical Problems of the Elderly*, Hutchinson.

HERON, A. (1963), *Preparation for Retirement: Solving New Problems*, NCSS.

HINTON, J. (1967), *Dying*, Penguin Books.

ISAACS, B., LIVINGSTONE, M. and NEVILLE, Y. (1972), *The Survival of the Unfittest*, Routledge & Kegan Paul.

KAPLAN, M. (1972), 'Implications for gerontology from a general theory of leisure', in *Leisure and the Third Age*, III International Course of Social Gerontology, Dubrovnik, International Centre of Social Gerontology.

KEAY, N. (1971), 'The home help in the Social Services Department', *Journal of the Institute of Home Help Organisers*, vol. 19, no. 53, June.

KERCKHOFF, A. C. (1964), 'Husband-wife expectations and reactions to retirement', *Journal of Gerontology*, vol. 19, pp. 510-16.

KNOTT, B. H. (1972), 'Social conflict: implications for casework practice', *British Journal of Social Work*, vol. 2, no. 4, Winter.

LAMERTON, R. (1973), *Care of the Dying*, Priory Press.

LITON, J. and OLSTEIN, S. C. (1969), 'Therapeutic aspects of reminiscence', *Social Casework*, vol. 50, no. 5, May, pp. 263-8.

LOWENTHAL, M. F. and BOLER, D. (1965), 'Voluntary vs. involuntary social withdrawal', *Journal of Gerontology*, vol. 20, pp. 363-71.

MARTIN, R. (1971), 'The concept of power: a critical defence', *British Journal of Sociology*, vol. 22.

MAYER, J. E. and TIMMS, N. (1969), *The Client Speaks*, Routledge & Kegan Paul.

MEACHER, M. (1970), 'The old: the future of community care', in *The Fifth Social Service: a Critical Analysis of the Seebohm Proposals*, Fabian Society.

MEACHER, M. (1972), *Taken for a Ride: Special Residential Homes for Confused Old People*, Longman.

MENZIES, I. (1961), *Social Systems as a Defence Against Anxiety*, Tavistock Pamphlet no. 3.

MILLOY, M. (1964), 'Casework with the older person and his family', *Social Casework*, vol. 45, no. 8, October.

MINISTRY OF HEALTH (1962), 'Development of local authority health and welfare services', *Circular 2/62*.

NATIONAL ASSOCIATION FOR MENTAL HEALTH (1972), *Mind Report No. 6*, May, NAMH.

NATIONAL OLD PEOPLE'S WELFARE COUNCIL (1967), *A Manual of Voluntary Visiting*, NCSS.

NATIONAL OLD PEOPLE'S WELFARE COUNCIL (1969), *Boarding-Out Schemes for Elderly People*, NCSS.

NEILL, J. *et al.* (1973), 'Reactions to integration', *Social Work Today*, vol. 4, no. 15, 1 November.

NEUGARTEN, B. L. (1963), 'Personality and ageing process', in R. H. Williams, C. Tibbetts and W. Donahue (eds), *Processes of Ageing*, vol. 1, pp. 321-34, Atherton Press.

PAPALIA, D. E., SALVERSON, S. M. and TRUE, M. (1973), 'Apprehension of coping incompetence and responses to fear in old age', *International Journal of Ageing and Human Development*, vol. 4, no. 2, p. 103, Spring.

PARKER, D. J. and FISH, S. S. (1971), 'Help for the home help service', *British Hospital Journal and Social Service Review*, 25 September.

PARSONS, T. (1967), 'On the concept of political power' in T. Parsons (ed.), *Sociological Theory and Modern Society*, Free Press.

POST, F. (1965), *The Clinical Psychiatry of Later Life*, Pergamon Press.

REICHARD, S., LIVSON, F. and PETERSEN, P. G. (1962), *Ageing and Personality*, John Wiley.

REID, W. J. and EPSTEIN, L. (1972), *Task-Centered Casework*, Columbia University Press.

REID, W. J. and SHYNE, A. W. (1969), *Brief and Extended Casework*, Columbia University Press.

ROBB, B. (1967), *Sans Everything: A Case to Answer*, presented on behalf of AEGIS, Nelson.

ROTH, M. and KAY, D. W. K. (1962), 'Social, medical and personal factors associated with vulnerability to psychiatric breakdown in old age', *Geront. Clin.*, 4, pp. 147-60.

RUDD, T. N. (1967), *Human Relations in Old Age*, Faber & Faber.

SAINSBURY, P. (1962), 'Suicide in later life', *Geront. Clin.*, 4, p. 161.

SHANAS, E. *et al.* (1968), *Old People in Three Industrial Societies*, Routledge & Kegan Paul.

SHANAS, E. *et al.* (1971), 'Disengagement and work: myth and reality', in *Work and Ageing*, 2nd International Course in Social Gerontology, International Centre of Social Gerontology.

SHAW, J. (1971), *On Our Conscience*, Penguin Books.

SKELTON, D. (1973), 'Comprehensive geriatric care in general practice. A possible organisational approach', in *Care of the Elderly*, Wessex Regional Hospital Board Working Party Report.

STANTON, B. R. (1970), *Meals for the Elderly*, King Edward's Hospital Fund for London.

STOICHEFF, M. (1960), 'Motivating instructions and language performance of dysphasic subjects', *Journal Speech Hearing Research*, vol. 3, pp. 75-85.

STORR, A. (1960), *The Integrity of the Personality*, Penguin Books.

SUMNER, G. and SMITH, R. (1969), *Planning Local Authority Services for the Elderly*, Allen & Unwin.

THIRD INTERNATIONAL COURSE OF SOCIAL GERONTOLOGY (1972), *Leisure and the Third Age*, III International Course of Social Gerontology, Dubrovnik, International Centre of Social Gerontology.

TIMMS, N. (ed) (1973), *The Receiving End*, Routledge & Kegan Paul.

TOWNSEND, P. (1962), *The Last Refuge*, Routledge & Kegan Paul.

TOWNSEND, P. (1963), *The Family Life of Old People*, Penguin Books.

TOWNSEND, P. and WEDDERBURN, D. (1965), *The Aged in the Welfare State*, Bell.

TUNSTALL, J. (1966), *Old and Alone*, Routledge & Kegan Paul.

WAGER, R. (1972), *Care of the Elderly—An Exercise in Cost Benefit Analysis*, IMTA.

WASSER, E. (1966), *Creative Approaches in Casework with the Aging*, Family Service Association of America.

WEBER, M. (1947), *The Theory of Social and Economic Organisation*, trans. A. M. Henderson and T. Parsons, Free Press.

WHITEHEAD, A. (1970), *In the Service of Old Age*, Penguin Books.

WILLCOCKS, A. J. (1973), *Which Way for Wardens*, report on a seminar on the role of the warden in grouped housing, *Age Concern Today*, no. 6, Summer.

WILLIAMS, E. I. *et al.* (1973), 'Socio-medical study of patients over 75 in general practice', *British Medical Journal*, 20 May, pp. 445-8.

WILLIAMSON, J. *et al.* (1964), 'Old people at home: their unreported needs', *Lancet*, i. p. 1,117.

WILSON, D. (1973a), 'Old Age', *Social Work Today*, vol. 4, no. 13.

WILSON, D. (1973b), 'Old Age, 2', *Social Work Today*, vol. 4, no. 18.

WOMEN'S GROUP ON PUBLIC WELFARE (1957), *Loneliness*, NCSS.

WOODMANSEY, A. C. (1972), 'The unity of casework', *Social Work Today*, vol. 2, no. 19, 13 January.

WOODRUFF, D. S. and BIRREN, J. E. (1972), 'Bio-feedback control of the E.E.G. alpha-rhythm and its effect on reaction time in young and old', *Proc. IXth Int. Cong. Geront.*, Kiev, USSR.

YOUNGHUSBAND, E. (1973), 'The future of social work', *Social Work Today*, vol. 4, no. 2, pp. 33-7, 19 April.